An Architect's Journals From Vietnam

1973-1975

PHILIP HENDREN A.I.A.

ISBN: 1492211281
ISBN 13: 9781492211280

ACKNOWLEDGMENTS

These stories would not have been given life without the help and encouragement of Mary-Helen Neville and Philippe Dambournet, who unblocked my memory wall about Vietnam. Her mom was one of the unsung heroines of USAID and an inspiration to us all. This project really began as Mary-Helen was going through the materials and photos that her mom had collected. Philippe's aunt/godmother was a friend of Mary-Helen's mom in Saigon, and her husband was a USAID colleague. This is our first attempt, and we are meeting weekly in hopes of doing a dozen or so pretty good stories. My thanks to them and also to my wife, Linda Humphrey, for her invaluable encouragement and proofreading.

*USAID is the United States Agency for International Development which operates subject to the foreign policy guidance of the President, the Secretary of State, and the National Security Council. It was created in 1961 by President Kennedy about the same time and with the same optimism that he created the "Peace Corps". It cracked open a door of exotic opportunity for many in my generation who took his "Ask Not" speech to heart.

BIBLIOGRAPHY

Barden, Thomas E., editor, *Steinbeck in Vietnam: Dispatches from the War,* University of Virginia Press, 2012. ISBN 978-0-8139-3257-6.

Fonda, Jane, and Tom Hayden, interview, *Playboy,* vol. 21, no.4, April 1974. A candid conversation with the activist actress and her radical husband, who helped found SDS.ISBN 1-57392-858-5.

Rubbo, Michael, writer, director, narrator, *Sad Song of Yellow Skin,* documentary film. 1970. ISBN 978-0-5200-4022-9.

Steinbeck, John Steinbeck IV, *In Touch.* Knopf, 1969. Library of Congress catalog #69-10685.

Steinbeck, John Steinbeck IV and Nancy, *The Other Side of Eden: Life with John Steinbeck.* Prometheus Books, 2001.

Thich Nhat Hanh, T*he Coconut Monk,* as told to Rachel Neuman, illustrated by Vo-Dinh Mai. Berkeley: Plum Bantam Books, 2009. ISBN 978-1-888375-97-8.

INTRODUCTION

In the summer of 1973 I was offered a "Peace Corp"-like consulting job to go to Vietnam as an "architect for reconstruction" of two university campuses that had been torn up by bombs. These stories are not about my architectural work but rather about my personal experiences with my co-workers and the Vietnamese people. Some of them are taken verbatim from the journals I kept.

By mid-April, 1975 the news from Vietnam was bleak and getting worse. I was worried about the people still there who had been my friends and colleagues during the previous two years. I had written to several and offered assistance and whatever help I might be able to provide. The Austin Statesman published an article with my picture with a group of orphans entitled "Austin Architect Hates to See S. Vietnam Fall" outlining my position on the state of the war and hope that the stalemate would result in something like what happened in Korea. I thought we had left the ARVN (South Vietnamese Army) powerfully equipped to defend themselves and my Vietnamese friends would somehow work themselves into positions of leadership in an emerging democratic republic of South Vietnam. I had only been back a few months and I had seen the vast acres of tanks, half-tracks, howitzers, jet-aircraft, ammunition dumps and what I thought was a well trained militia able to utilize all that equipment. Little did any of us know that within a few weeks, by April 25, the whole picture would collapse into a chaos of total defeat for all of the Americans still there and all the Vietnamese civilians who had been our friends and allies.

It was a two-year life changing experience and when I returned in late January, 1975 I was blind-sided by the realization that the American people were so war-weary that no matter who you were or what you had done, nobody wanted to hear anything bad or good about Vietnam. I put my photos and journals in boxes and clammed up. It is now forty years later and the first time that the boxes have been opened and some of stories relived.

John Steinbeck IV at Phoenix Island, 1968.

JOHN STEINBECK IV & THE ISLAND OF THE COCONUT MONK

"Have you seen the Island of the Coconut Monk?"

It was the first question I was asked when Dr. Mary Neville, our division chief, introduced me to her friends and USAID staff as an architectural consultant in Vietnam to help with the reconstruction of two university campuses that had been damaged by the war. I had just arrived from Hong Kong, and like most Americans I knew almost nothing about Vietnam except what I had learned from participating in antiwar protest demonstrations and from horrendous TV images.

It seems that in 1968, a French-trained engineer and worldly Buddhist monk named Dao Dua had set out on a one-man peace mission to try to end the war and provide a safe haven for military deserters from both sides on an island in the Mekong River.

This "Coconut Monk" had enlisted the aid of a famous American architect named Paolo Soleri from his Frank Lloyd Wright–inspired enclave near Phoenix, Arizona. Soleri was building an ambitious planned community named Arcosanti and was famous for supporting his operations by teaching his architectural student interns to make cast-metal bells to sell to visitors. Not surprisingly, the two apparently collaborated well and saw the possibility of creating a "peaceful haven" in the middle of the war zone and supporting it with "swords-to-plowshares" projects.

For example, used howitzer shells could be hammered into attractive and marketable objects like bells and flowerpots. The gong they used to summon all the disciple monks was made from the end of a five-hundred-pound bombshell.

Together, Dao Dua and Soleri created a sort of "Delta Disneyland" with space age–looking towers, a sunny pagoda with helipad, and totems with modest religious overtones. They dubbed their site Phoenix Island and proceeded to build a facility that could accommodate American, Communist, and Saigon dignitaries to meet and settle the problem of peace in Vietnam. Dao Dua managed enough political clout to persuade all opposing armies to respect the neutrality of Phoenix Island since there were conscientious objectors from both sides present. (The island was never attacked.)

I had never heard of the Coconut Monk or Phoenix Island, but I had not only heard of Soleri, I had been to Arcosanti, had met him, and had studied his work since I was an architectural student. I certainly wanted to visit the Island of the Coconut Monk!

OFF-LIMITS

It wasn't possible to arrange an official visit to the monk's island because it was unexplainably listed as "off-limits" to US personnel. I suppose it carried this designation because it was protecting military deserters and didn't officially exist. Darrell Dawson and Bob Craine, veteran USAID consultants who were my first friends in the country and my guides to the mysterious streets of Saigon, both told me not to worry: "We do stuff that's 'off-limits' all the time." They both spoke street Vietnamese and were invaluable to me. Things we did that were "off-limits" included:

1. Shop in the "black market," the only place one could buy hand tools, office supplies, electronic products, fresh groceries that were supposed to go to the PX, the latest American popular music on cassettes, and so on.

2. Catch rides in the local taxis. We were supposed to take State Department limos, but it could take hours waiting for one. (Happily, I was soon assigned my own jeep. However, it was almost impossible for me to find an address in the big city by myself.)

3. Visit the resort city of Vung Tau, the closest beach and a famous R and R retreat for GIs.

4. Visit so many restaurants and bars that pretty soon one learned not to even ask—instead, just go for it. Anyway, by the time I arrived in Vietnam there were no longer many MPs in town.

So the next week, my Vietnamese counterpart, an architect named Mr. Ngo Viet Thu, met with me and discussed including a trip to Phoenix Island as part of my introduction to Vietnamese architecture. An excellent companion, he had studied at École des Beaux-Arts in Paris and was the first Asian architect to be chosen as a honorary fellow of the American Institute of Architects (AIA). He had designed the University of Hue's campus, which was one of the sites I had been hired to help restore and repair.

We had to drive to the small village of My Tho and a small wharf on the banks of the Mekong River where we hired a water taxi. It was a small boat with a direct-drive engine that hung precariously off the stern. It looked like a ten-horsepower lawn-mower engine that was rope-started and had a twenty-foot-long pipe with a swivel mount. The drive shaft went through the pipe and had a simple three-bladed propeller at its end. The driver simply grasped a U-shaped handle on the motor and pointed the drive shaft to control the direction and speed of the boat.

Mr. Thu said he couldn't actually visit the island with me, but he could get me there and wait for me with the boat at the landing. It was close to midday and about two miles to the island. It was wonderful to see the lush tropical jungle bordering the Mekong. At one point our boat passed under some low-hanging coconuts, so our driver called out to the lady on the bank to see if we might buy some. She smiled and motioned for us to bring them to her. She picked up a machete and expertly cut and punctured the fruit so we could drink the milk while her three kids watched. The coconuts were delicious, and the kids thought I was very funny.

The arrival at Phoenix Island turned out to be at the Coconut Monk's large houseboat (a floating pagoda) that was permanently docked and served as the entrance and the modern kitchen facilities for the entire island. We were immediately invited for lunch on the top deck, but Mr. Thu explained that he had to stay with the water taxi. He introduced me as an American architect who just wished to visit. Present were one thousand or so people of all ages and about three hundred disciple monks, most of them Vietnamese military deserters from both sides. The floating pagoda was recognized as a sanctuary, and the governments of both North and South Vietnam maintained a "hands-off" policy.

Lunch on the pagoda was a simple but tasty rice and veggie dish, and the chopsticks were beautifully carved. I was seated at a table, but most of the disciple monks sat cross-legged on the floor and ate very slowly with serious deliberation as if savoring every morsel in a spiritual manner. Several kids sat near me eyeing my Nikon.

My guide, who had reported my arrival to Uncle Hai (the Coconut Monk), came to say that there was to be an assembly of all disciples in the public arena and that I was the guest of honor. The monk had decided to break his vow of silence so that we could exchange greetings publicly over a PA system with translators. (He normally observed a two-hour period of silence from noon till two o'clock.)

There were two towers rising from the floating pagoda, one said to represent Saigon, the other Hanoi. An elaborate architectural model of the area sat between the towers, showing buildings, jungles, rivers with houseboats, farms, mountains, etc. It was said that the monk made daily symbolic trips between the towers in an effort to promote peace through a kind of "conflict-resolution meditation." Each day after his two hours of silence, he would carefully move among the pathways between the towers searching for a "path to peace." He truly wanted to become known as the monk who brought peace to Vietnam.

There is a Buddhist teaching that embodies the use of "visualization with icons." It was explained to me that you sort of build a model either physically or in your mind of a resolution to the conflict. This "resolution model" then becomes your "mantra" or daily routine that you can work on and refine. The physical model helps both parties see the problems and work them out. This is an amazing idea to me, sort of like saying, "Here is how architects would go about designing the ending of a war"!

The monk was barely visible to me as he sat at the top of the "Saigon" tower on a raised dais. I stood in front of a microphone at the top of "Hanoi" as he welcomed me to his sanctuary in Vietnamese and said that he loved architecture and hoped I would like his structures and designs. It was an artful maze of Buddhist totems and colorful ornaments. I said I was most impressed with the imaginative towers and especially liked the bridges.

He asked that I carry a message to President Nixon, inviting him to meet with all hostile parties at this location and hold direct negotiations under the Coconut Monk's auspices. He felt if he could just get the conflicting parties to his island to experience his "path to peace," they would find the way. The primary goal was to achieve peace and a satisfactory cease-fire. What was amazing was that he had miraculously created a facility, including a heliport, right in the middle of a war zone, one that really could facilitate such a peace conference!

I said I would gladly convey his invitation to President Nixon at the earliest possible time. The throngs of disciples applauded loudly, and I felt like the future of this horrible conflict now had been laid in my lap.

That night back at the US Embassy in Saigon, dinner was served family style to encourage embassy personnel to exchange the events of the day. (Since everything was winding down, I had been assigned to the guest room where Secretary of State Henry Kissinger had stayed.) At my table was US Representative Bella Abzug and her assistant, an attractive lady about my age. I knew Bella had fought for civil rights, civil liberties, and peace in Vietnam and, even better, had shattered the tradition that freshmen members of Congress don't make waves. I was frothing to tell her what I had done that day, but I couldn't say a word because you really don't talk about stuff you do that is "off-limits." It wasn't too difficult remaining quiet because she really wasn't a good listener and wanted to do all the talking about how we should get out of this mess.

Her assistant, however, seemed as glad to see me as I was to see her. I told her that I had had the most incredible experience that day and would love to tell her about it in private. She said they would love it if I could come to their guest room after dinner for a drink.

We had an hour or so back at her room before Bella could tear herself away from the dining room, so I told her the whole story. It took about half a bottle of excellent scotch, but she said she loved my story and promised to get the message to Bella and to President Nixon. I knew it might be the scotch talking, but it was my best shot at helping find an end to what had become America's darkest hour.

Two years later, after recovering (somewhat) from my refugee-rescue adventures after the fall of Saigon in the spring of 1975, a call came in from the University of Colorado at Boulder offering me a job teaching design in the School of Architecture. They had no idea how broke and distraught I was at the time, and I didn't tell them, but their offer of a new location and great salary seemed like manna from heaven. I learned right away that no matter who you were or what you had done, nobody in the country wanted to hear anything about Vietnam!

But that is how I happened to be in Boulder that next fall, and I wandered into Le Bar at the Boulderado Hotel. It was sort of Boulder's version of that bar in *Star Wars* with all the weird animals, so it became my favorite hangout after school.

Thanks to Watergate and the dramatic fall of President Nixon, my father and I had mended fences; my father even apologized for backing such a scoundrel for so long and said he really respected the things I (we) had tried to do to help the Vietnamese people. Anyway, we met in Boulder late that summer, and he helped me with a down payment on an unfinished condo that a bank had foreclosed on. The deal included a huge pile of tongue-and-groove oak flooring that the builders had intended to use. Since I didn't want to buy furniture, I decided to build everything I needed out of the leftover oak. All I bought was a doggie bed for Dudley, my English sheepdog mix, and a king-size waterbed.

One evening I showed up at Le Bar in sawdust-covered overalls from doing carpentry. I seemed to fit in better with the weirdos and hippies than I did in my school clothes. Anyway, one of the regulars had noticed my beat-up Land Rover with Dudley sitting behind the steering wheel and asked if it was my rig. I admitted it was, and we had a drink or two. He turned out to be one of those rare individuals who make you feel you could say or do anything and he'd understand and approve. He was eager to match me weirdness for weirdness, so we began to compare notes.

We'd both had difficult fathers with whom we recently reconciled, so we drank to that. He said that Dudley sitting out there in my heap (land yacht) reminded him of Charley, the dog his father had written a pretty famous book about. I said, "You mean *Travels with Charley*? That was your pop?" Yup, turned out I was sitting there with John Steinbeck IV, and I had just read that book. What's more, I had just traveled from Austin to Boulder with Dudley! So we drank to that. He said, "I have an aunt in Austin, maybe you know her. Name is Liz Carpenter, who was LBJ's press secretary for a while." I said, "Don't know her, but one of my friends is Molly Ivins, and she thinks Liz Carpenter is fabulous." So we drank to Liz and Molly.

As I was leaving that night, John walked me out to the truck and noticed it was crammed with tools and stuff. He said, "I'd really like to learn how to do some carpentry. Could I come help you?" We were both a little stoked, but I said, "Sure, I think that would be great. I get home from class around four," and I gave him the address. I figured it was just the booze talking, but the next day around four thirty there he was, six-pack and a few cigarettes in hand.

He loved working with the tongue-and-groove oak boards. We would slide them together to make planes that we would then sculpt with a big power sander to make a kind of fireplace surround and sitting area. We had so much oak we could be really extravagant and make little storage crannies and bookshelves, etc. He'd never even hung a door, so all this was new to him. I was glad to have the extra hands.

One day after we found out that we'd both been in Vietnam, I asked him if he'd heard of the Island of the Coconut Monk (aka Phoenix Island), and I told him my story and the message for President Nixon. To my shock he said, "Holy ______, I know you! I remember you! I was there that day!" He went on to tell me how he had returned to Vietnam after his hitch was up in the army. He was in love with a beautiful Vietnamese lady and wanted to work as a free-lance journalist. He had actually started a news service called Dispatch News Service along with some other guys including Sean Flynn, son of the famous actor Errol Flynn. He and Sean would go over to Phoenix Island to escape the chaos of the streets of Saigon and for glimpses of the truth about what was really happening with the war. They both studied Buddhism and became friends of the monk.

So it turned out we really had a lot to toast as we nailed and glued and sculpted a fortune's worth of oak flooring.

Around 1967, President Johnson was struggling to find a way out of the war and out of the pressure he was getting from the antiwar demonstrators. To try to sway public opinion, he invited John Steinbeck (at the time the only Nobel Prize–winning author in the United States) to the White House. He knew Steinbeck had a son in the army, and he wanted Steinbeck to go to Vietnam to tour the war theater, visit his son, and, hopefully, return with enough positive material to write a series of articles for the *Newsday* magazine to counter the arguments of the antiwar protesters.

John IV told me that his dad considered LBJ a friend, so he did it—or tried to. After the first or second article was published, the *New York Times* panned him for abandoning his liberal past and taking up lopsided pro-war views. For that and other reasons, like finding out there were 150,000 ex-GIs organized against the war, he had a complete change of heart and tried to prevent *Newsday* from publishing any more of his pro-war articles. John IV said he couldn't prove it, but he would always believe that the stress over that situation caused his father's heart attack and death in 1968.

Here's the thing...perhaps the Coconut Monk, Dao Dua, didn't succeed in bringing the war to an end, but his peaceful island haven certainly provided a refuge for John IV, Sean Flynn, and others while they were organizing the Dispatch News Service (DNS). Probably the single most powerful news story that influenced American public opinion and shortened the war was Seymour

Hersh's November 1969 account of the My Lai massacre when American GIs murdered an entire village—published first by the DNS! No other event had such clout in convincing Americans of the insanity of this conflict, and it may never had been uncovered had it not been for John Steinbeck IV, Sean Flynn, the Coconut Monk, and others at the DNS. This Pulitzer Prize–winning story gets my vote for the most important piece of journalism in the twentieth century. Certainly Dao Dua and the Island of the Coconut Monk deserve recognition for being the environmental backbone in the creation and support of the DNS.

The author in Saigon, summer 1973.

Architect Ngo Viet Thu, my friend and guide, on the way to visit the Island of the Coconut Monk. He spoke both French and English and was a graduate of the École des Beaux-Arts in Paris. He had designed the campus in Hue that we were working to restore.

At one point our boat passed under some low hanging coconuts, so our driver called out to the lady on the bank to see if we might buy some. She smiled and motioned for us to bring them to her. She picked up a machete and expertly cut and punctured the fruit so we could drink the milk while her three kids watched. The coconuts were delicious, and the kids thought I was very funny.

Coconuts on the way to the Island of the Coconut Monk.

The Buddhist monk Dao Dua, the Coconut Monk, was a former well-to-do French-educated engineer. Born Nguyen Thanh Nam, he established a religious community on Phoenix Island in the Mekong River that drew from Buddhist, Taoist, and Christian traditions. He was imprisoned a number of times by the government for preaching his pacifist beliefs and advocating the peaceful reunification of North and South Vietnam. It was believed that he subsisted as a coconut vegetarian, that is, on nothing but coconuts. The barge "pagoda" held two towers with flags representing Hanoi and Saigon. The monk was seated cross-legged in one tower with his pet bear and monkey, and I was invited as the guest of honor to the top of the other tower. The "bombshell" gong was rung to summon all the disciples for a PA-system exchange between us. He apparently knew an architect would be impressed with his constructions and creative efforts. He was right! (Years later I learned that John Steinbeck IV was there that day and remembered it well.)

Every day the Buddhist disciples chanted and prayed for a meaningful cease-fire and a peaceful solution. Phoenix Island attracted hundreds of followers and became a haven for those attempting to escape the ravages of war, including Vietnamese peasants and American soldiers.

Dao Dua on Phoenix Island. Each day he would make a symbolic journey through the model of the landscape between the two towers representing Hanoi and Saigon in his meditative search for a "path to peace."

John Steinbeck IV at Phoenix Island, 1968.

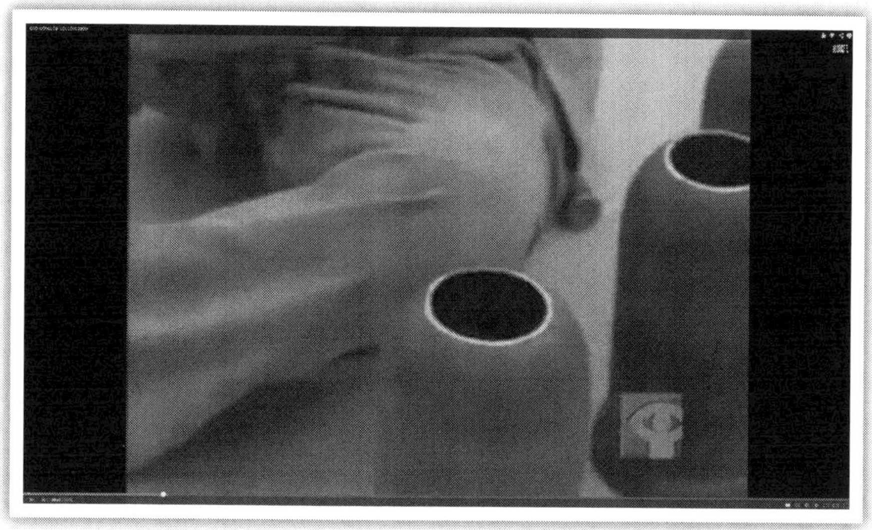

The scrap howitzer shells became bells or flowerpots.

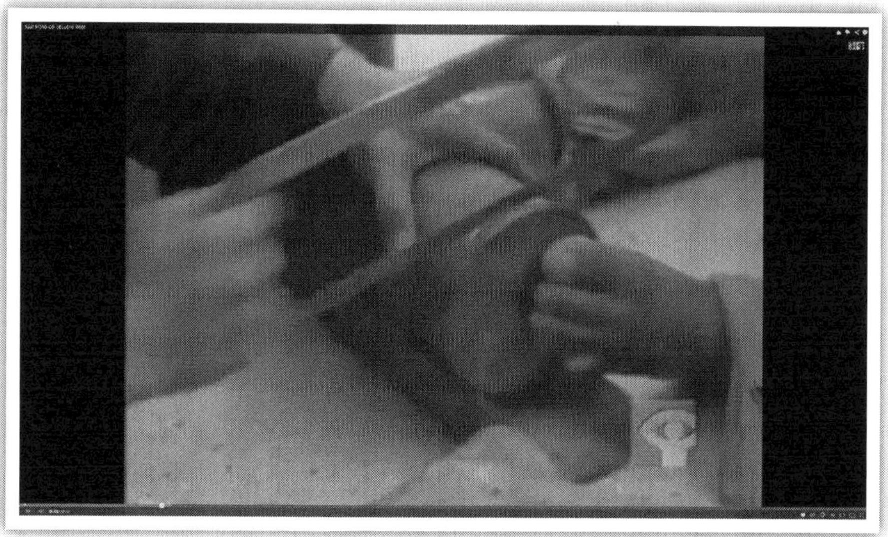

The scrapped war material became useful using simple hand tools.

The gong in the center, made of a bombshell, was rung to call the disciples.

A Soleri bell from Arcosanti. The Coconut Monk enlisted the aid of the famous American architect Paolo Soleri from his Frank Lloyd Wright–inspired enclave near Phoenix, Arizona. Soleri was building an ambitious planned community called Arcosanti and was famous for supporting his operations by teaching his architectural student interns to make cast-metal bells to sell to visitors.

Phoenix Island was the only place in Vietnam where one could find happy Vietnamese thriving in a bizarre colorful environment. John Steinbeck IV, Sean Flynn, and other free-lance journalists went there to interview ex-soldiers from both sides and gather material for the Dispatch News Service. The stories that emerged played a significant role in shortening the war.

HOA·HIEP TON·GIAO XA

LUCK OR JUST GOOD KARMA?

Setting: Late summer, 1973, at a cocktail party at Dr. Mary Neville's apartment, Saigon

INTRODUCTION

One of the greatest things to learn about the human race is that whenever you are on a mission to do something "high-minded," "worthwhile," "truly idealistic," or "heroic," people seem to appear out of nowhere to help.

By Friday of my second week, I had visited both campus sites and met with my Vietnamese counterpart, architect Ngo Viet Thu. He was a tall, attractive, truly cultured gentleman and an excellent architect who had won the prestigious Grand Prix de Rome and had designed the University of Hue campus, which had recently been leveled by the US Air Force. Helping to rebuild it was one reason for my being there. Mr. Thu spoke four languages, and we loved to communicate design ideas with sketches, so we got along immediately. (My oversized business card was a sketch pad that went everywhere with me.) He seemed genuinely happy to see me because my predecessor in this job, Professor Harry Ransom of Rice University, had given him glowing reports about me. Harry and I were great friends, and he was the one who got me into this and told me about Mr. Thu, who would be my guide and translator.

Mary had arranged an end-of-the-week cocktail party so I could meet some other USAID consultants and people she knew who could help us get things done in this confusing place at this confusing time. Our primary job was to reassure the South Vietnamese of our support in the event of a casualty of war—in this case two university campuses. Apparently, the US political policy was, "Okay, so the VC destroyed some university buildings, killed some of the faculty and some students. . .we refuse to allow this to stand! The classes will continue, they will meet in outdoor classrooms or under improvised shelters, each faculty member that is missing will be replaced with a 'suitcase professor' from the University of Saigon whose salary and transportation needs will be met by USAID!"

When we visited the campus sites this is what was happening. They were using bombed-out shells of old brick classrooms and roofless spaces with blackboards on easels and mats on the floor. The jungle and tropical plants recover so quickly that it was actually a quite pleasant environment. We later attended the graduation ceremonies of the University of Hue—the first graduation in six years!

Mary, my boss, knew that the war was not over yet and that our Seabees or someone was going to be building these things we were talking about in a DMZ, which didn't exist. I still hadn't got my head around the scope of the problem. Do you rebuild what was there? Do you build concrete bulletproof bunkers and line them with sandbags? Do you build temporary thatch and bamboo classrooms and provide underground bomb shelters? Will our campus turn out looking like a walled-in army base or a prison with guard towers on the corners? (I leaned toward the thatch and bamboo option.)

At the party, Thu and I needed to pin down some design concepts. While we were sketching and talking, Mary came over to listen in and offer suggestions. When she saw some new guests arrive, she said, "Oh, you two have to meet this couple. He is the head of the Ford Foundation here, and she is his assistant and an English professor at the University of Saigon." The reason we should meet them, Mary said, was because there was a new Ford Foundation–sponsored campus and school in Bangkok. It might point in a useful direction since the climate and materials were similar to what we would find in Vietnam—albeit without a war. I loved her positive attitude. So it was that in a couple of days I was off to Bangkok to learn what I could about Southeast Asian contemporary campus design.

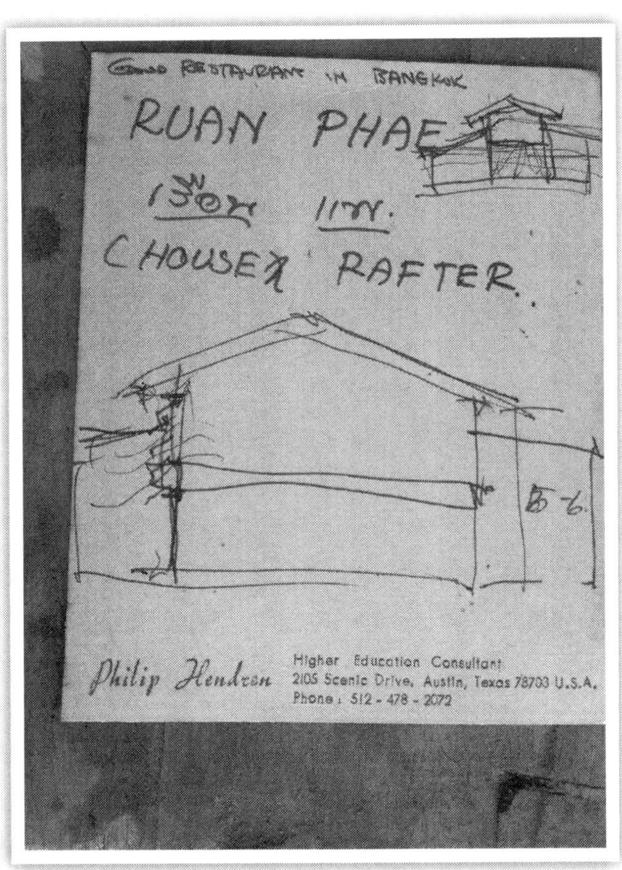

Thailand was a great role model for what South Vietnam could become. The Ford Foundation had sponsored a program where professional artists, designers, and craftspeople from around the world were offered one-year fellowships to come to Thailand to help local talent develop products for the world market. With the indigenous materials and pool of Thai talent, it had been extremely successful, especially in the world of textiles and wood products. There was no reason that the same kinds of things couldn't happen in the new South Vietnam. I thought it sounded perfect and exactly the concept we needed for the design and planning of two new university campuses.

Mary's party was an interesting mix of local artistic and intellectual talent. Guests included:

- Mr. T. C. Clark, US ambassador to Vietnam
- Robert and Vicky Trott, director of CARE (Vietnam), building 150 refugee houses
- Rosemary Taylor, head, Vietnam Adoption Agency, New York City
- Colonel Wendy Niblo (ret.), volunteer and director, An Loc Orphanage, Saigon
- Mr. Do Ba Khe, minister of education, Vietnam
- Mr. Bob Craine and Mr. Darrell Dawson, engineering consultants, USAID
- Nguyen Kim Tuan (Duy Lam, pen name), well-known author now in charge of new Da Nang University

- Bob Van Horn, USAID consultant, former Peace Corps volunteer
- Mr. Andy Andrews, head of Air America
- Dr. Heaston Rothwell, former president of Mills College and head of Ford Foundation, Vietnam

There were also two Korean gentlemen who had recently arrived to oversee the import of hundreds of mopeds as part of President Johnson's effort to stimulate Vietnamese cooperation. (The idea was to give them what they want and need and then we'll have a powerful bargaining chip.)

I thought to myself, "Well, this is certainly one mighty cultured group of folks. Wonder if I really belong?" I said something to that effect to the two Koreans, and one responded, "Our prep school tutor said there are five requirements for one to become a 'truly cultured gentleman.'" I thought uh-oh, so I said, "Indeed, and what might those be?" He then listed the five requirements:

1. Speak at least two languages.

2. Play at least one musical instrument.

3. Know the words and sing at least one song.

4. Recite at least one poem.

5. Prepare and serve at least one tasty meal with the proper wine.

Let's see, I thought, I'm pretty fluent in English and Spanish, there's the guitar and harmonica, I can play and sing "Hawaiian Beach Boy," I know the words to Dylan's "Blowin' in the Wind" if they press me for a poem, and I can cook coq au vin in a wok with Chardonnay. I just hoped they weren't going to ask me to prove it tonight!

There were two folks, Curt and Polly Schneider, admiring one of Mary's paintings by a local artist, so I said that something about the style of the artist, whose name was Becky, and her mastery of the brushstroke reminded me of Chinese calligraphy. We had a nice chat. They were living in Bangkok where he was a zoologist with the Smithsonian and she was teaching at Mahidol University.

When I mentioned I was going to Bangkok the next day, they suggested I might like to attend an art opening on Saturday by a Thai artist whom they were very fond of. They wrote his name in my diary—Thawan Duchanne, known as "Tuan"—and the gallery, the Mekpayab Art Centre on South Sathorn.

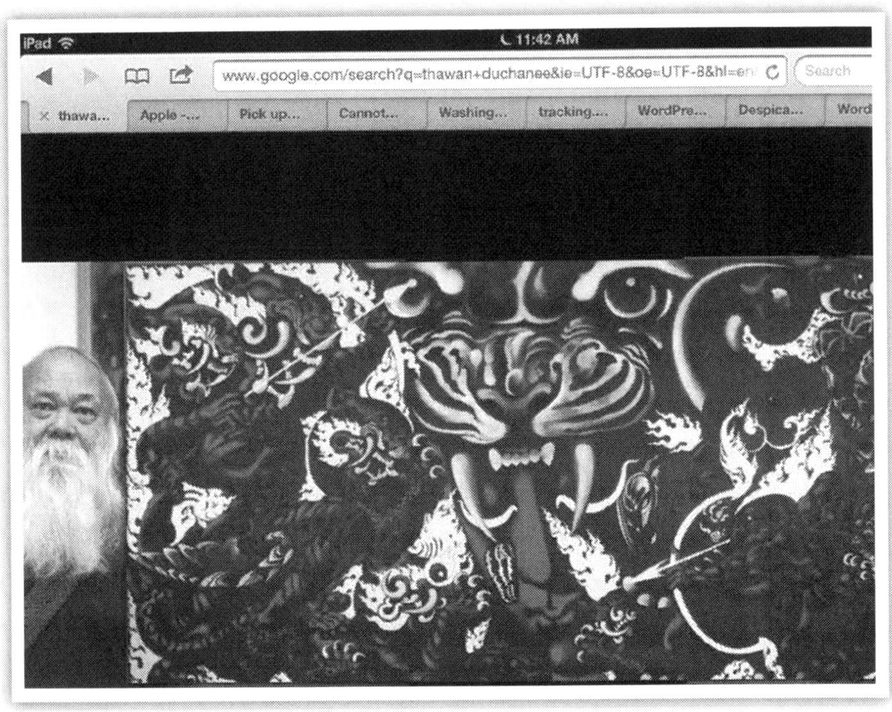

Thai Artist "Thawan Duchanne," aka "Tuan"

The next evening in Bangkok at the hotel, I asked the concierge to ask the cab driver to take me to the Mekpayab Art gallery. It was a cocktail opening and quite crowded, but the paintings were excellent and I could see why my new friends loved this guy. The mix of people reminded me of New York, and I was impressed that Bangkok was so different from Saigon. I met "Tuan," who was very gracious, and I told him he had some great admirers in Saigon. He said yes, they had recently purchased some of his work.

As I was about to leave I noticed a tall, slim, European-looking blond lady standing alone, admiring a large oil painting. I thought,

"Sure wish I could speak French," but I went over anyway and said hello.

She smiled a little. I said, "I think this guy is really good!" She smiled again and said, "I agree. It's the only thing I've seen in Bangkok that I really love," in a perfect south-central Texas drawl! She was not French at all. Her name was Pina Indorf from Cuero, Texas, and like me, a graduate of the University of Texas in architecture. She had joined the Peace Corps and was posted in Thailand.

When I told her what I was doing and why I was in Bangkok, she said, "Maybe I can help. My best Thai friend is also a UT graduate and is head of development and facilities planning for the Thai Ministry of Education." What a fortunate chance meeting! She offered to bring her friend Malinee to my hotel the next evening so we could meet. I went back to my room feeling that my lucky rabbit's foot must be working overtime, but the name Malinee nagged at me and kept nagging all night.

The next afternoon around four I was waiting in the hotel bar when in walked two smiling ladies carrying a heavy parcel. It was a 1962 (remember, this is taking place in 1973) University of Texas yearbook, the *Cactus*, with Malinee's finger holding a place in the book. Without saying a word she opened the book and pointed to a picture of the two of us in a portrait of the student chapter of the AAAE (American Association of Architectural Engineers) of which I was the president. We had been great friends, and I had picked her up at her dorm and given her a ride to all the AAAE meetings that school year. Needless to say, she made my visit to Bangkok very pleasant and productive.

Front Row: Hendren, Terry, Galbraith, Wheeless, Fox, Spencer, Sagarik, Cruz, Wolf, Ma
Second Row: Falkenberg, Abraham, Popkin, Hanson, Schodek, Buckner.
Third Row: Lile, Kueck, Nichols, Oxford, Hendrickson, Ashland, Friedrichs, Woytek.

OFFICERS

This photo is the American Assoc. of Architectural Engineers from the University of Texas "Cactus", 1962. That's me on the left and my friend Malinee Sagarik from Thailand on the front row. Finding her in Bangkok was miraculous and her help proved invaluable.

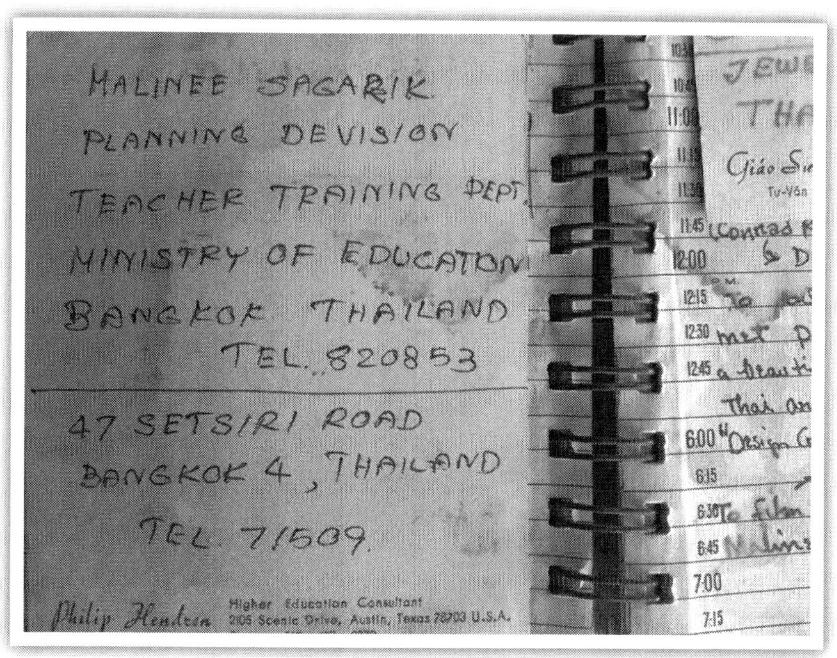

A page from my journal with Malinee's address in her writing. She provided the information I needed for my proposals for the new universities in Vietnam.

Pina Indorf, fifth from left in top row. She was in the Peace Corps in Bangkok and meeting her at the art gallery was either "good luck or good karma"! This Photo from the School of Architecture class of 1962 University of Texas *"Cactus"*, yearbook, but I had not known her then.

Malinee wanted to show me some fine teak furniture, so we went to an open-air market—unbelievable! Besides the furniture, there was a cobra and mongoose fight! In a large caged in arena, the cobra was coaxed out of large wicker basket by a swami sitting cross-legged and playing a flute. The mongoose was the crowd's favorite but neither won, so I guessed that they would need to fight again the next day. There were dozens of orchids totally new to me and sweet coconuts (rum optional). It was such a wonderful place that I wondered why our shopping malls back home couldn't be more like this.

Our next stop was to visit a Mr. Larry Carlson on Rajavith Road, head of the Peace Corps for Bangkok. He was also Pina's friend, and they thought he was really current on how to get things built in Southeast Asia. In my diary/sketchpad I wrote, "Must See: 1. Jim Thompson (Thai Silk), 2. Star of Siam (textiles), 3. Design Thai, (art and jewelry), 4. Thai Lapidary (stones)."

The next day we went to the Silpakorn University School of Architecture and met a professor of Thai architectural history who generously gave me a copy of a student thesis titled "Design Criteria for Tropical Architecture." From this material I formed a set of ideas on how to proceed in Vietnam; for example, "We must somehow tie agricultural industry to the building industry. For instance, I saw building panels made of compressed rice hulls. Furniture should be specifically designed for non-air-conditioned spaces. Lighting should all be twelve-volt bulbs and solar powered."

Malinee mentioned that there was yet another UT School of Architecture graduate I should meet, Phisit Phisitthakorn. He was her great friend and lived on the river in a classic exotic Thai house that she said I must see. The house belonged to Princess Chumphot, who was one of the prominent art collectors in Thailand. (The famous Marsi Gallery in the Chumphot Pantin center for arts is named for Marsi Paribatra, the daughter of the princess.) The Prince and Princess Chumphot had given the Krishnavana House located at 777 Bang Plat, Thonburi, to a well-known American scholar, Dr. A. B. Griswold, in appreciation for his having written an excellent set of volumes on the history of Thailand. I said, "Sure, let's go!"

She called Phisit and he said, "Great, come for lunch. We'll eat on the river." So we went to a Perfume River taxi stand because the only way to get to Krishnavana House was by river taxi. The Perfume River in Bangkok is the spinal cord of the city. It simply makes the city work, like the canals of Venice, and I loved it. When Phisit said, "We'll eat on the river," he meant we would sit under an umbrella at the end of the dock, and small boats with ladies with delightful foods would come floating by. That's exactly what happened. They could have accurately renamed it the Gourmet River.

Phisit was an architect with a huge international corporation called Borneo Engineering Co. Limited on Nares Road in Bangkok. He had lived in Austin for five years for his degree and was a good friend of his thesis adviser, who was also my friend and colleague, Dr. Hugo Leipsinger. Phisit was one of those rare individuals born with a perfect body and perfect posture, but I decided to like him anyway. He drove a new Volkswagen but kept it in a garage, so mostly we went by river taxi. He said that since Dr. Griswold was in Washington for the next few months that they would be honored if I would move from my hotel and be their houseguest. He said he had already spoken to the princess and that she would love to meet me. We should plan to meet her at Thai Lapidary that day at four. My thought was, "What do I say to a princess?"

Krishnavana House on the Perfume River was traditional Thai architecture and inspirational! It boasted floors never touched by shoes and teakwood floors like the deck of a ship. Fans were arranged to move air over fountains and pools built into the perimeter. Exotic fish were in ceramic waist-high ceramic pots. They were a sideline business for Phisit. He insisted I go with him on a fish-buying mission on Saturday morning when the river was lined with merchants for every conceivable need you could imagine. He fed the fish until they quadrupled in size and then returned to market to trade for even more exotic babies. When I woke up the next morning, the thought crossed my mind that maybe this wasn't real; I might have died and found myself in heaven! Happily it was real, but I began to feel that somehow I was going to have to pay for all this good luck! I borrowed a book from the library entitled *Afterthoughts on the Romanization of Siamese* by A. B. Griswold.

Malinee took me to her home where her mother ran a small restaurant, and I met her large family. She took me to a Thai greenhouse where her uncle bred orchids with almost the same fervor that we breed racehorses. She was a dancer in a traditional Thai dance company, so Pina and I attended its performance. In addition to all that, Malinee supplied more documents than I needed for my mission and the report I would write.

Pina and I loved hanging out with Malinee, but she had her work duties so we headed off on our own to explore Bangkok. Pina had been the only woman in her graduating class in the School of Architecture at UT about 1963. The profession at that time was so male dominated that it was difficult for her to find a job. She recalled, "A job? I couldn't even get an interview!" That was what led her to join the Peace Corps. But she really loved it and was happy to be in Bangkok where there was lots of work and a booming economy.

When I told her I was interested in using Thailand as a role model for the design and exportation of goods for the world market, she took me to a company in Bangkok named Molinox.

The company had been inspired by the Ford Foundation initiative and had developed a line of teakwood furniture that took into consideration the problems of overseas shipping. An agricultural consultant in Saigon had told me that the Vietnamese lumber industry was shipping tons of raw log lumber to Japan. He had proved that if they would first convert the logs to wood products, the value of the material would multiply by a factor of thirteen! But most fully assembled furniture is simply too bulky for efficient container box shipping. No one had yet worked out designs that could be shipped with practically no dead air and then assembled at the destination point by the buyer. Molinox was doing this with teakwood furniture designs that used mortise-and-tenon joints that needed no glue and were simple enough to be assembled by the end user. I decided to propose a Molinox-like operation for Vietnam.

A week in Bangkok and it seemed my life was charmed and things were falling into place. I now thought I finally had a concept for what to do. However, I had to get back to war-torn Saigon, and Malinee insisted on taking me to the airport. She insisted that we first stop at a special Buddhist temple where the monks had a special ceremony for ensuring the safety of departing travelers. Part of the ceremony included the traveler buying (for about one dollar) a cage of birds. Then after a short prayer and a bit of arm waving, the traveler would open the cage door and the birds would fly away, taking with them any worries or fears one might have. (They flew to a particular place in the hills above Bangkok where kids would catch them and then bring them back.)

So I purchased a cage with three birds. Holding it high above my head, I opened the cage door. The birds fluttered away, but alas, one of them flew directly into the closed window of a parked taxi. It fluttered to the ground and Malinee rushed over, carefully picked it up, and held it close to her chest. She patted its little head and said, "I think he'll be okay, but Philip, you must not fly today. This is bad omen."

So, no argument here, I enjoyed an extra day in Bangkok and went with Phisit to trade exotic fish. I called Malinee, and she said the bird had recovered and flown away before she could get to a vet. When my plane landed in Saigon, I rubbed my rabbit's foot again and wondered if I really could remember the words to "Blowin' in the Wind."

OFF LIMITS

Setting: Mid-February, 1974, Vung Tau, Vietnam,

The Author in "Vung Tau, Vietnam, 1973.

Perhaps the strongest pull to get me to want to go somewhere is to declare it "off-limits."

My flight arrived in Saigon at 8:45 a.m. on February 16, 1974. I was met by Bob Craine, Darrell Dawson, and George Marlowe. When I asked how things were going since my last visit, Marlowe said, "No problems that required anything more than patience." On the ride into Saigon they were filled me in on all of what was now "off-limits" to American personnel. It was like a list of all the things we should plan to do because they were fun, exciting, and probably a little dangerous. I learned on my previous visit that if you honored the "off-limits" directives you would get basically nothing done.

The following comes verbatim from my diary:

"Lunch with Bob Craine interrupted by emergency closing of restaurant—mysterious but rather exciting, thought for a while we might be under siege—probably just a police raid...new crackdown on bars, etc. by Saigon police and this restaurant usually has topless waitresses—mysteriously missing today. Went to two bars just to celebrate my return...the girls are still beautiful and loving. Everything same as six months ago but piaster now worth 565. Word is that Mary [Dr. Mary Neville, my boss and head of USAID/Education] and most USAID people will be out by mid-April."

The point is that even though almost all the GIs had gone home, the war was not over and the South Vietnamese army was notorious for misrepresenting the truth about how the war was going. For example, the following appeared in that day's English newspaper at the US Embassy guesthouse:

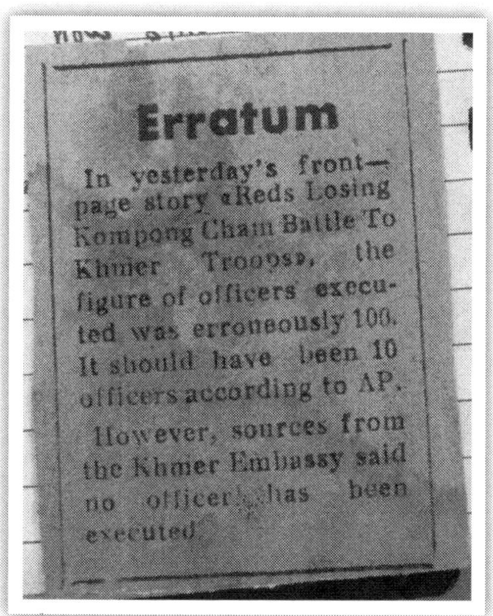

Erratum

In yesterday's front-page story «Reds Losing Kompong Cham Battle To Khmer Troops», the figure of officers executed was erroneously 100. It should have been 10 officers according to AP.

However, sources from the Khmer Embassy said no officer has been executed.

These "errata" appeared nearly every day in the only English language newspaper in Saigon. Some were even more tragically hilarious than this one!

"Whatever the case, few analysts, with the exception of the ever optimistic US Embassy, held much hope for the current regime."

And from my issue of *Time* magazine:

"It is too late to even hope for a coalition arrangement. The other side holds all the cards now. It is only a matter of time to see how they play them."

Anyway, I was really glad to see these guys since they had been vital to helping me complete my mission the previous year. Two university campuses, one in Hue and one in Can Tho, had been battlegrounds during heavy fighting and suffered extensive damage. My work had been the planning and design for their restoration and remodeling. It required utilizing the resources of USAID and Air America ("CIA Airlines") and the FAC (Forward Air Control) so we could get aerial photos of the sites, etc. Craine and Dawson both spoke street Vietnamese and knew many tricks for short-circuiting red tape and getting vital supplies and services (sort of like Radar in *M*A*S*H*). With their help, I was able to present a set of realistic proposals. These led to my being invited to return by the rector of the University of Can Tho.

High on the list of "off-limits" things we should do included a visit to Vung Tau.

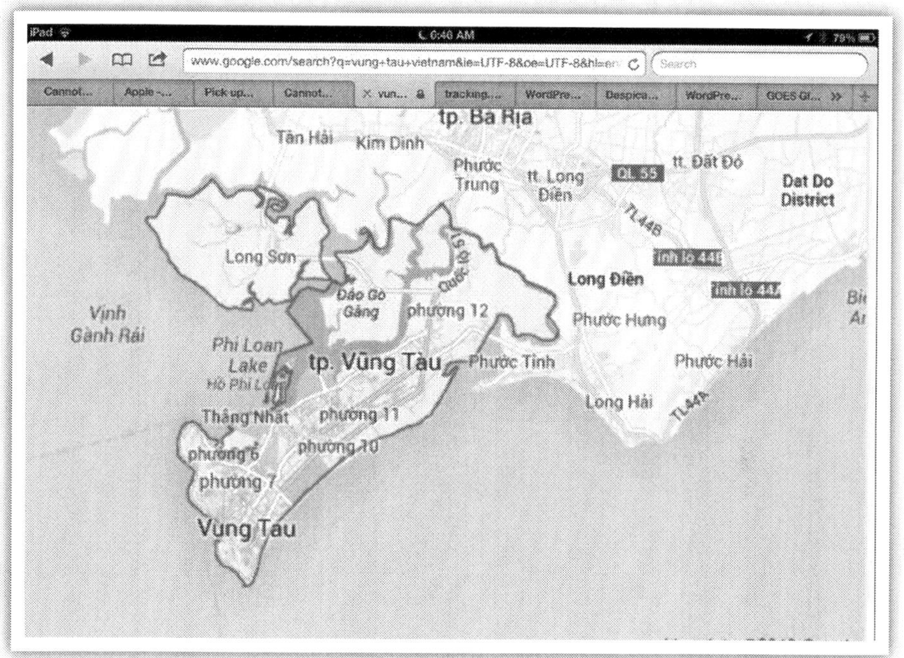

Vung Tau was the major staging area for the Australian army and they loved it. It was by far the best R&R place anywhere in Vietnam and it being made "off limits" just made it all the more desirable that we go there.

Vung Tau is a small tree-shaded village about fifty miles south of Saigon with beautiful, white sand beaches. It was the major staging area for the Australian army, which had been by far our most helpful and reliable ally during the worst periods of the fighting. They were now gone as were our GIs, but it had been one of their favorite R and R destinations. Gambling was openly allowed, and the main drag looked like a small Las Vegas strip with bright flashing lights and bars (saloons) with names like "OK Corral," "Trader Joe's," "Golden Nugget," "Stardust," etc.

From left top: Darrel Dawson, Bob Craine, Hang, Ye Thuong, and their two Vietnamese friends in Vung Tau.

Note the wonderful "S" shaped fenders made from ammonia impregnated plywood.

There were wonderful two-wheeled, one-horse carts for hire for sightseers like us, so we hired three and set off to tour the area. Note the craftsmanship of these chariots and the S-shaped fenders of plywood. One couple could ride in each cart while the driver stood behind on a step with a buggy whip. The small but spirited horses loved to run full out, so before long we were galloping lickety-split around the plaza. It was easy to see why the GIs loved this place!

Craine's love and feisty lady friend, Hang (flowered hat and sunglasses in the photo), had introduced me to her friend Ye Thuong, who lived in Saigon but had grown up in Vung Tau and seemed very comfortable with the horse carts (called *xe ngua*). On the way to the beach we stopped for mangoes on the side of the road. Later on a beach towel, Ye borrowed my boot knife and carefully sliced a mango into three sections, leaving the oval seed in the middle. The two outside sections were like long, fat canoes, and she delicately cut the yellow meat into square grids without touching the skin. She then flipped and folded the fruit into a pretty Popsicle-like flower and showed me how to hold it and eat the cube sections without getting them all over my face or clothes. She was very shy about speaking English, so it was all done without a word. I was totally charmed. Her smile was as delicious as the mango, and I wondered how many more things we could do that wouldn't require words?

Cutting a mango is truly an art form and one of the best skills I acquired in Southeast Asia.

On the beach we watched an ancient but fit old guy twirling a small fish-shaped wooden object over his head like a cowboy with a lariat. When the circle widened to about twenty feet, he flung it with great body strength far into the surf. He then moved back and forth like someone flying a kite. After several casts and to everyone's great surprise, he pulled in a sizable white fish that had swallowed his little wooden lure. I had to go closer, so I walked over and smiled and bowed as he worked the lure free and handed the fish to the small boy who I guessed might be a grandson. I pointed at the lure, and he handed it to me for closer inspection. It was about six inches long and made of *cao*, an Asian hardwood heavy like our walnut. It was fish-shaped and had holes at each end but no hook, which I was expecting. I was impressed that such a simple tool could yield such a catch! Apparently his lure looked enough like a small fish wiggling in the water that a bigger fish would just swallow it.

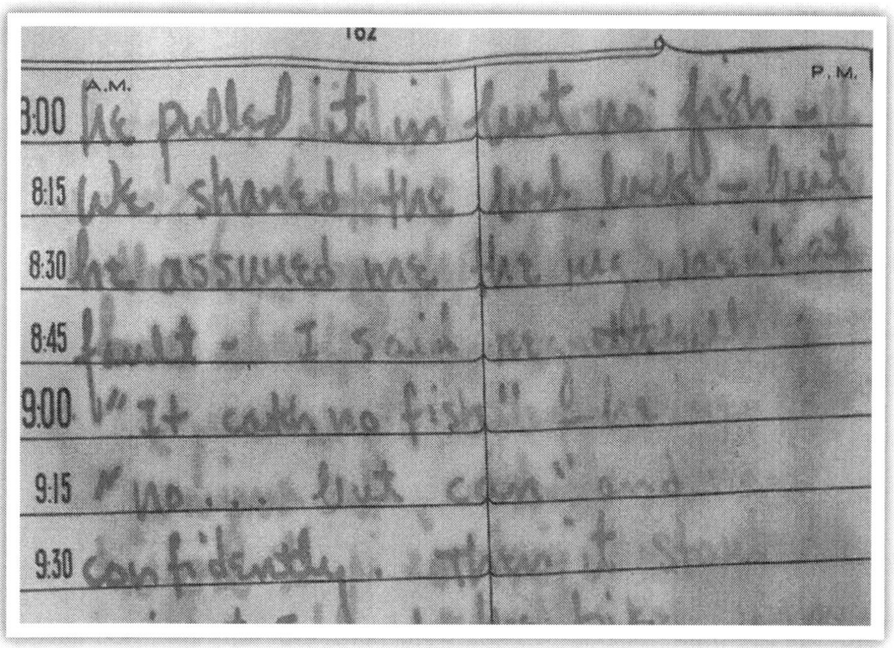

102

A.M. P.M.

8:00 he pulled it in but no fish

8:15 We shared the bad luck – but

8:30 he assured me the net wasn't at

8:45 fault – I said [illegible]

9:00 "It catches no fish" [illegible]

9:15 "no [illegible] but can" and

9:30 confidently [illegible] then it [illegible]

There were other locals fishing with nets, mostly women and small kids. They would gather in a circle with a large circular net that had baseball-size stones sewn into its perimeter. They would then wade far into the surf and with great teamwork fling the net as far as they could until it landed and sank. Then, by pulling on the perimeter cord, they could gather the stones into a clump and pull up whatever happened to be swimming under their throw. On one occasion they found two jellyfish among a large number of small fish and communicated an alarm by frantic hand waving. They carefully avoided the tentacles of the jellyfish and netted them with small handmade landing nets that were on hand for the occasion. They then waded ashore and killed the jellyfish with rocks. It seemed barbaric to me, but I had never been stung by a jellyfish; apparently it is excruciatingly painful! They were very happy to have gotten rid of them. The fish they caught were dragged up to a paved area and arranged in a big grid to be cleaned and dried in the sun. We saw several pallets of these on sale to villagers. Apparently after a few hours in the sun they are simply eaten with no further cooking required.

After our delightful picnic on the beach, we went exploring for shells and to have a look at an ancient warship that had beached on the reef. Before we got there I noticed another mystery that had to be investigated and unraveled. There were about ten large hardwood logs that had been hollowed out somewhat like canoes. They were sitting on stout sawhorse things that seemed well anchored into the rocky beach near the water's edge. When I asked, I was told it was a salt factory! Everybody but me seemed to know how this ancient method of salt collecting worked. It is beautifully simple. The tide comes in, filling the logs with saltwater. The sun evaporates the water and leaves crusts of valuable sea salt. Teams of kids come along with bamboo spatulas and scrape the salt into bags. It's a wonderfully efficient system dating back hundreds of years. (It is interesting that there many different kinds of sea salt, depending on which sea it comes from. The most valuable is a red sea salt, which comes from the coral reefs off the surf in Hawaii.)

These ingenious traditional methods made me wonder what if anything they might have to do with how the Communist Viet Cong had the hell bombed out of them, yet they were still coming on strong. Many of their rules for guerrilla warfare were taken from Sun Tzu's *The Art of War,* written before the time of Christ! The idea of defeating a modern army, navy, and air force with tunnels and sharpened bamboo sticks seemed preposterous, but then so did catching a big fish with a piece of walnut! How little we knew then how close we were to disaster in this area.

In my quarters in Can Tho at a guarded military encampment called Palm Springs in the middle of the Mekong Delta, there were stacks of paperback books left by the former GI occupants. Among them were pamphlets that had been issued to arriving servicemen describing various booby traps being used by the VC. They were pretty beastly, and they invariably utilized simple materials such as sharpened bamboo, gravity pits, knowledge of the enemy (e.g., How far up does a combat boot protect the leg of a soldier? Make your spring trap hit above that), clever trip wires concealed in spider webs, and many more diabolically conceived tricks. Later I found out that General Westmoreland not only knew of *The Art of War,* but also had found translated excerpts and issued them to all US officers and platoon leaders. The original work from 2,500 years ago was translated by Samuel B. Griffith. Amazing is that many of its principles are still applicable today.

Since we were "off-limits" and didn't want to be traveling back to Saigon after dark, we cut our beach time short and hopped on our one-horse chariots for the gallop back to town. Ye Thuong asked our driver to take us to the home of her family for a quick visit since it was close to where we had left our van. When we arrived she was shocked to see her father, Mr. Bay, sitting head-in-hands on the curb outside the family business/home compound. It turned out to be an enterprise for repairing, restoring, and selling the *xe ngua* buggies like the ones we were sitting on. She climbed down to see what had happened.

Vietnam is primarily a matriarchal society with the women managing the purse strings and pretty much controlling the family purchasing power. The rationale seemed to be the men are simply too generous and tender hearted, and if the money was left to them they would give it to their friends or to the needy or squander it in some way. In this case, it was payday, and her father had visited a casino after work and the week's wages had been lost. Consequently, her mother had banished him from the house and was not speaking to him.

I said, "Gosh, that's awful. What can we do? I'll be glad to loan him some cash." Ye said, "No, he won't take it." Then I noticed the large barn doors opening as one of the employees was leaving, and inside there must have been twenty or so carriages in all states of condition; wheels and harnesses and tools and parts were hanging from the rafters. I hopped down, and Mr. Bay perked up at my interest in his shop. We were introduced, and while Ye and Craine translated I told him I was an American architect and explained what I was doing in his country. My card told him in Vietnamese that I was a *kien-truc-su* (architect) with USAID. I admired the craftsmanship of these chariots and asked how they made the S-shaped fenders of plywood. We were invited into the shop, and he showed us the area where they impregnated the plywood strips with anhydrous, or pure, ammonia and then used a printing press–like thing to shape the fenders. (The ammonia turns wood fibers into something like rubber for a short time.)

I was still worried about helping him with his current predicament, so I said, "How much would it cost to buy one of these?" He said something like, "We have many. Which one do you like?" Our driver was still waiting outside, so I said, "How about that one?" He said, "About 140,000 piasters" (roughly $250). I said, "Okay, deal!" But I had only about $150 on me, so I said, "Here's a down payment," and handed him the cash, figuring that would be that and I would at least get him back in the house. Ye took the money, and soon we were all invited into the parlor to meet the whole family. They asked us to stay for supper, but we had to make a quick exit to get back to Saigon before dark.

I knew buying that thing was silly, but since I was getting "hardship pay," it had only cost about a day's wages for me. I just chalked it up to a good deed and part of the cost of a fun day in Vung Tau. (Also, I got a tearful smile and big hug from Ye Truong—a name that translates "easy to love.")

Fast forward to four days later. I was in my VIP guest room at the US Embassy in Saigon when a marine guard knocked on my door. He said there were a couple of Vietnamese guys outside the gate who wanted to see me. Ye's father, Mr. Bay, and her brother and a small horse had walked with the *xe ngua* from Vung Tau to Saigon and were delivering the shiny red classic one-horse cart. They had simply shown my card to the guards at the gate. I had to jump in my jeep and go to the bank to convert a hundred dollars into 56,500 piasters. (The money filled two grocery bags.) When they finished counting, they brought the *xe ngua* onto the grounds of the Embassy and unharnessed the horse under a big shade tree. It sat there for the next three months and was much admired by all. I never had to explain exactly that it had come from a wonderful "off-limits" place.

How it got back to Texas is another "off-limits" adventure.

The *xe ngua,* at our place in Austin. I wasn't able to restore the S-shaped fenders, but all the other parts are original.

THE JOURNEY TO HUE

Setting: Spring 1973, Saigon/Hue, South Vietnam

The helicopter was a small bubble-top four-seater.

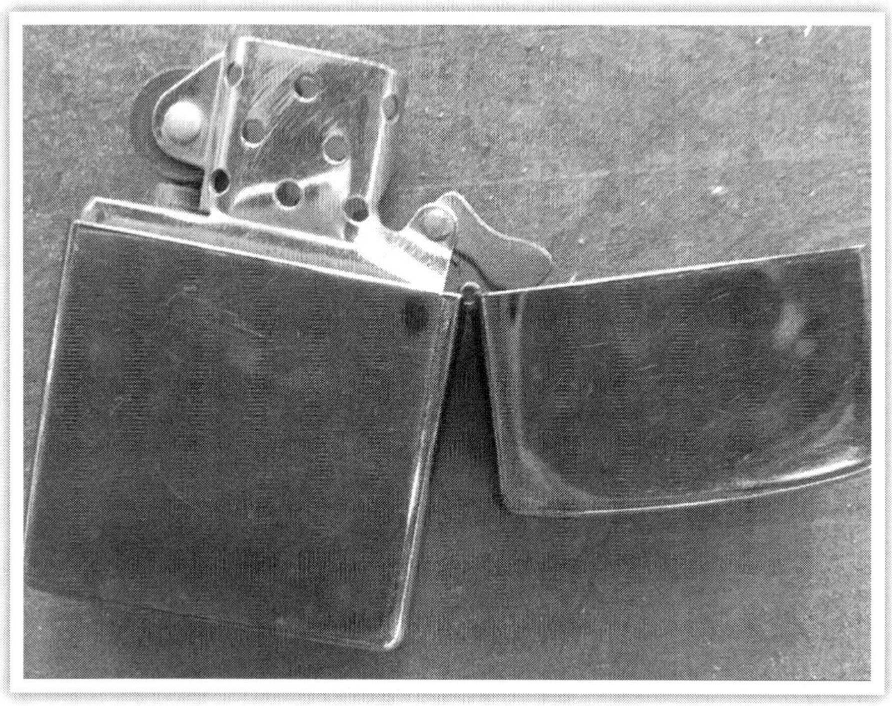

Zippo
Premium
Lighter Fluid
Cleaner Burning
Improved Ignition
Low Odor

The Zippo lighter: it has been a legend among servicemen since World War II.

Every time I run across one of those Zippo lighters, I can't forget the time one of them nearly ruined the day and then miraculously saved the day. The Zippo has been a legend among servicemen since World War II and may even have been government issue to all GIs during that war. Even in Vietnam the Bic disposables hadn't quite arrived, and the familiar snap of a Zippo had almost the feel of a gun cocking. Opening or closing it was about half the fun of smoking.

If an attractive woman in a bar approaches you for a light even today, it is by far the best response to pull out and open up your Zippo lighter! Anyway, it was the end of the semester in the spring of 1973, and we had to get from Saigon to Hue to attend the first graduation of a class from the University of Hue since the war started.

Most people don't realize that the universities and their faculties in South Vietnam were the first targets of the Communist Viet Cong, which regularly kidnapped whole student bodies and faculties. The classrooms and laboratories were usually destroyed or damaged by Allied forces in extricating the enemy. Therefore, for a class of students to have made it through four years for a graduation was truly miraculous and a testament to at least one success of the USAID efforts to accomplish something worthwhile. Since Dr. Mary Neville was USAID chief of education and had been pivotal in getting that university back on its feet, she was to be the guest of honor. Her daughter, Mary Helen, and I were just going along for the ride.

Mary Helen awaiting our much-anticipated trip to Hue.

Since the VC were still blowing up bridges and marauding convoys on the road between Saigon and Hue, our only choice was to go by Air America, (aka "CIA Airlines") helicopter. The three of us arrived at a desolate beachside landing pad near Saigon and waited to be picked up. (I have to say, the Air America guys were excellent pilots and really helpful in ferrying me around the campus sites where we were designing repairs and renovations. Later they turned out to be true heroes in helping Americans and hundreds of Vietnamese friends and employees escape as Saigon was falling.)

The helicopter arrived at the appointed time and we piled in. It was a small, bubble-top four-seater, so Mary Helen and Mary hopped in the back, and I got in the copilot's spot. When I noticed a thumb-size hole in the center of my bucket seat, the pilot grinned and pointed to a corresponding hole directly above that had been repaired with duct tape from the outside. He said, "That's why we don't fly direct to Hue from here. Too many jungles, and the VC snipers are pretty good. Just lucky nobody was in that seat on our last trip!" So we took off due east over the beach intending to fly the whole distance over water since Hue was also a coastal city. The surf was heavy and we were flying lower than I would have liked, but I guess a sniper on a surfboard wouldn't be much of a threat. Still, there was that hole I was sitting on.

The sliding cockpit windows were ajar, giving us some relief from the heat with the ocean breezes. Our pilot pulled out a package of Winstons and stuck one in his teeth and offered me the pack. I declined, still thinking about the hole. He then pulled out his Zippo with his right hand to light up, but the small gale kept blowing out the flame. I was thinking, surely he's done this before. So he casually let go of the stick so he could shield the flame long enough to light up. Naturally, the spring-loaded stick returned to its base position, and the craft began a rapid nose dive toward the surf. The Zippo flamed out again and our guy cussed the wind and grabbed the stick just in time to pull us back to level—much to our relief. I was thinking that maybe he did this all the time to liven up a boring flight, but I was afraid to look back to see how the ladies were doing. His second effort was a repeat of the first, so I finally grabbed the lighter and said, "Here, let me try. Maybe I will have a smoke after all." This time the Zippo lasted through two lightings and I thought, "Gee, what a great design!" Happily, we didn't have to swim to Hue, and the whole thing gave new meaning to the expression "smoking can kill you."

Our pilot pulled out a package of Winstons and stuck one in his teeth and offered me the pack.

At the time, the best book on the war in Vietnam was *Fire in the Lake* by Francis Fitzgerald. I had skimmed it, but a friend who had been there for several years jokingly said he was working on a sequel called *Fizzel in the Lake.* (Both had a lot to do with the difficulties of finding any truth about what was really happening.) Thinking of this, I wrote in my diary that maybe I should write a story entitled "Fizzle in the Helicopter."

We made it to Hue unscathed, and it was wonderful seeing the site that we were to be working on from the air: beautiful scenes of peasant lifestyle along the rivers, an enviable easy existence with plentiful fish, rice, bananas, coconuts, etc. It was hard to see the effects of the war from there, but on closer inspection there were scenes of total desecration, probably the work of our C-47s nicknamed "Puff the Magic Dragon." They were the Douglas workhorses of World War II equipped with three six-barreled Gatling guns, which stuck out of two side windows and the open door. In a dispatch to *Newsday* on February 25, 1967, John Steinbeck wrote, "…these three guns can spray out 2,800 rounds a minute—that's right, 2,800. In one quarter turn, these guns fine-tooth an area bigger than a football field and so completely that not even a tuft of crabgrass would remain alive."

Apparently, the US political policy was, "Okay, so the VC destroyed some university buildings, killed some of the faculty and some students; we refuse to allow this to stand! The classes will continue, they will meet in outdoor classrooms or under improvised shelters, each faculty member that is missing will be replaced with a 'suitcase professor' from the University of Saigon whose salary and transportation needs will be met by USAID!"

When we visited the campus sites this is what was happening. They were using bombed-out shells of old brick classrooms and roofless spaces with blackboards on easels and mats on the floor. The jungle and tropical plants recover so quickly that it was actually a quite pleasant environment.

The following is from my diary:
"Hue, June 1, 1973: In Hue at the hotel we sat in the rooftop outdoor restaurant overlooking the Perfume River listening to the distant mortars or rockets. I thought the red light was fire or napalm but its persistence revealed it was red lighting; probably from parachuted flares. There is a

certain romantic nonchalance about calmly eating under the stars while war rages in the distance. Maybe the sounds of bombs at that distance are surrealistic reminders of life's shortness, kind of acoustic markers of hours passing. I thought of a news item that day where a career air force pilot had refused to fly another B-52 bombing mission and instead he jettisoned his bombs out over the ocean. I guess he wanted to join the GIs against the war movement but at any rate the story seemed to indicate he would be court-martialed and it would ruin his career. When I mentioned this to Bob Van Horn (longtime USAID veteran) at breakfast, he said, "Shoot, if he didn't want to hurt anybody he should've just flown the mission as prescribed. The missions are known many days ahead and we even drop leaflets announcing their location and time; if anyone stays around and gets hurt it's their own damn fault! If you drop bombs over the ocean you might accidentally hit some poor fishing boat or something. This guy just wanted out and was making a statement." I thought about that when I heard the bombs that night and hoped that Van Horn was right.

"It grew almost cold in the night and the bombs quit, but the mosquitos were unmerciful. In this sparsely populated country human blood must be a rarity. We were a seldom-found dessert to them, and they whooped and attacked, power diving and wheeling up and diving again. The visibility was good and we made excellent targets. Only when we got back to the motorcycles could we get away. Thankfully our mosquito nets were tightly tucked around our beds and we could get to sleep with less fear of malaria; however, I still slept fully clothed in some fashion.

Graduation ceremonies at University of Hue, July 25, 1973:

(July 25, 1973)

OPENING ADDRESS OF THE RECTOR OF THE UNIVERSITY OF HUE

(English Translation)

****

Ladies and Gentlemen,

It is certainly an honor for the University of Hue to welcome all of you to the Graduation Ceremony of the 1972-73 academic year. On behalf of the entire staff of the University of Hue I would like to convey my heartfelt thanks to all of you who have come here today to participate in this ceremony and to witness the graduation of those who have completed work for their degrees.

On this occasion I would like to ask you to allow me to look back on the road that the University of Hue has traveled during the past few years, more specifically from the tragic days of the 1968 Tet Offensive to the present time.

This University, situated near the front lines of battle, has had to live through a turbulent period of history, has had to survive many political and military crises, and, as if these were not enough, has also suffered from natural disasters such as typhoons and floods. The result of this has been that the University of Hue has been continually damaged- both spiritually and materially. The sixteen years that the University of Hue has been functioning have been years of trial and tribulation.

One of the most difficult trials that the University of Hue has had to face was the Tet Offensive of 1968. This tragedy presented the University with certain problems that had to be solved. During the three weeks of heavy fighting, the University suffered heavy damage. University offices, classrooms, laboratory equipment, libraries, books were all destroyed but of course the hardest loss of all to bear was that resulting from the deaths of teachers, students, and administrative staff members. This destruction was so cruel in its intensity that many people thought that the University of Hue could never recover. But thanks to the resilience and persistence of the Vietnamese people, thanks to the enthusiastic assistance provided by the Government, the special support of people in this region, thanks to the valuable aid offered by international organizations and friendly nations, and especially thanks to untiring efforts on the part of the entire staff of the University of Hue, the material destruction was repaired and the University was rebuilt very quickly.

But it was not enough to simply repair the material damage and rebuild the physical plant of the University, for the 1968 Tet Offensive had repercussions not only in regard to physical facilities; there was tremendous destruction caused in the realm of the spirit as well which amounted to what can be called a crisis in confidence. After the physical destruction, after the tragic, senseless killing which occurred during the three weeks of fighting, many people returned in a state of abject despair, completely devoid of confidence both in themselves and in the future. And in any educational endeavor the one thing which is absolutely essential is confidence. And because confidence was lacking, suddenly suspicion and divisiveness appeared. Therefore it was decided that if the University of Hue were to continue to operate, it had to analyse again what its goals were, decide again the direction in which it should head, and establish a program for development which would reduce this suspicion, bridge the gaps between the different factions, and search for a way to bring about a renewal of confidence in the minds of students, teachers, and the administrative staff. If this is to be done then the educational goals of the University of Hue must be appropriate to the realities of the present situation and effective in satisfying the development needs of the nation and the local community. Every teaching endeavor and every research project of the University must take as their starting point the realities of Vietnam today. They must draw their vitality from the needs of the nation, the local community, and the student body.

Of course the goal of "the University serving the community" spoken of above is not the only goal of the University of Hue. The University has no intention of abandoning such goals as the dissemination of knowledge, the development of culture, the spreading of understanding and international cooperation. However, during the present period, of all the goals of the University of Hue this goal to serve the community has become the most important, has been given the highest priority.

If we take this goal "To Serve the Community" as a yardstick with which to appraise the various educational activities of Vietnamese universities, we must be frank and admit that the curriculum and method of teaching is too remote, too far removed, from the existing realities of the nation and the local community. The problems that are brought forth to be researched or to be taught are not really related to community needs. And the pressing problems of the community are not taught or studied at the universities. The result of this is that the universities do not contribute anything to the development of the nation or the local community because what the students who graduate from these universities know does not suitably equip them to be able to respond to the needs of the community. The cause of this situation is perhaps the tendency of the universities to lay too much stress on the theoretical teaching of literature, philosophy, and other liberal arts subjects drawn from the treasure house of national and European and American culture. In the process the teaching of practical things related to present day life in the surrounding community has been forgotten.

Actually the educational situation described above is an old fashioned model of university education which was introduced into Vietnam a long time ago by the Western nations. Today the Western nations themselves also must conduct a reappraisal, must readjust this model, so that universities can play a part in the solving of the practical problems of the community. Complaints have been raised against this kind of university education which in past years has not contributed anything to the community nor benefited the student in any significant way. Since the curriculum is too abstract, the knowledge which a student picks up in the school of books is of no help to him in the school of life; the student's abilities are too limited to enable him to make an effective contribution in the task of national and local development. In addition the learning environment has been too narrowly defined, involving as it has simply the dimensions of the classroom or the laboratory. Therefore the student feels very far removed, feels bewildered, when he enters the school of life. And finally, the methods both of teaching and learning that have been employed have been too passive. Students have studied in order to pass their examinations, in order to become academicians of the type that regard their university degree as a privilege, not as a responsibility which is owed the community. While students are in school the universities fail to inculcate them with a concern for the problems of the nation, for the needs of the community. Therefore students fail to become imbued with a sense of responsibility in regard to community problems and are unwilling to effectively involve themselves in the life of the community.

It is to remove the deficien-cies that I have just described that the University of Hue in recent years has made every effort to reorient that part of the curriculum which has been in existence for some time and at the same time to introduce some new features to the curriculum which are more practical but still embody the highest cultural and spiritual values. All of these efforts have had as their aim the making of university education of more benefit to the community and to the student. To completely realize these programs the University of Hue needs a staff of high quality and quantity.

But procuring staff members has been one of the most unsolvable problems of the University of Hue. Because of its location near the front lines Hue has become the most uncertain and eventful place in Vietnam. In addition, natural disasters such as typhoons and floods often descend upon Hue. For these reasons the cultural, economic, and commercial life of the city has been severely curtailed. This in turn has a tremendous affect on the circumstances which a teacher or administrative staff member finds himself in and has turned his life into a difficult struggle to make ends meet. If one compares the standard of living and working conditions of the members of a university in the capital with those in Hue one will see that they vary considerably. It is precisely for this reason that it has become so difficult to invite teachers to come to Hue to teach on a full time basis. Even the problem of getting teachers presently teaching in Hue to stayin Hue has proved to be unsolvable!

The above address by Rector Truong provided exactly the philosophy and fodder I needed to formulate a master plan for the university's new campus. I totally agreed with his concept of an institution to serve the needs of the community and to get away from the old-fashioned model of university education that was introduced into Vietnam a long time ago by Western nations.

I found and sketched a fisherman's house on a tributary of the Perfume River, which I felt incorporated many features we could utilize in the new campus designs for both housing and classrooms. I felt that if we could incorporate indigenous materials and self-reliant energy systems such as solar and wind, we could build a model that could not only serve the needs of the university but the community as well. The new ideas could be made to work smoothly with the traditional.

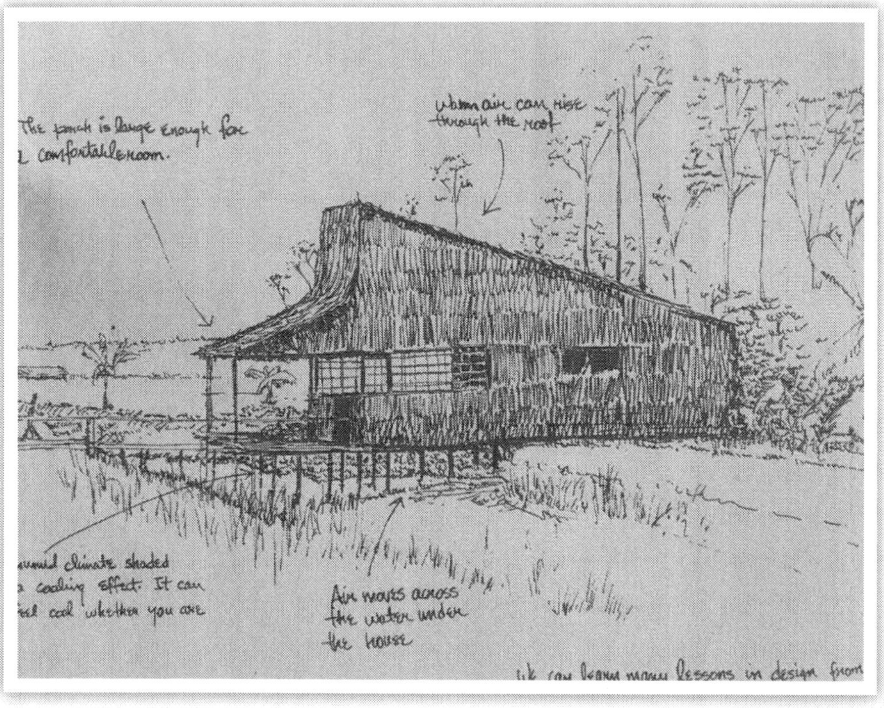

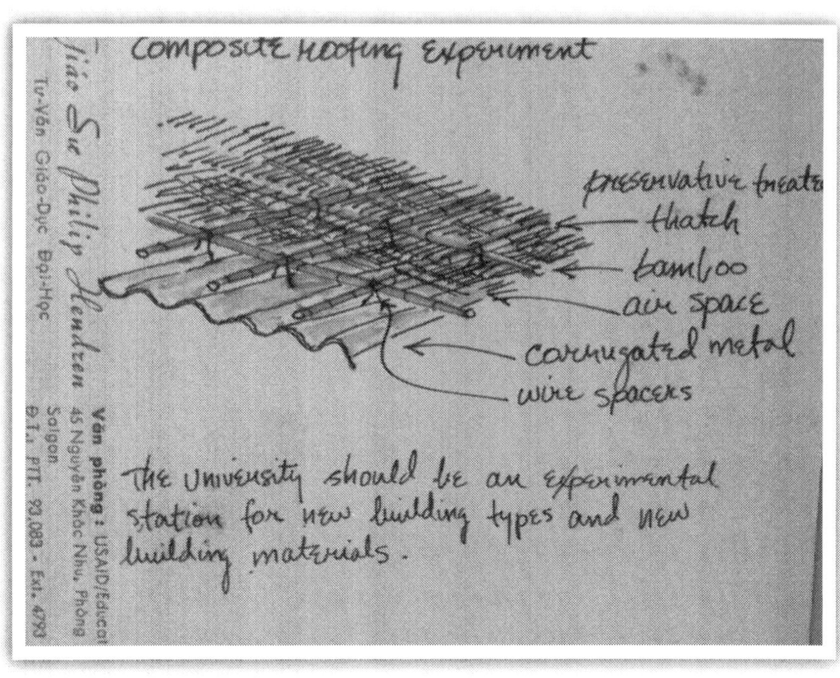
Composite roofing experiment
preservative treated
thatch
bamboo
air space
corrugated metal
wire spacers
The university should be an experimental station for new building types and new building materials.
Giáo Sư Philip Hendren
Tu-Vấn Giáo-Dục Đại-Học
Văn phòng: USAID/Educat
45 Nguyễn Khắc Nhu, Phòng
Saigon
Đ.T.: PTT. 93.083 - Ext. 4793

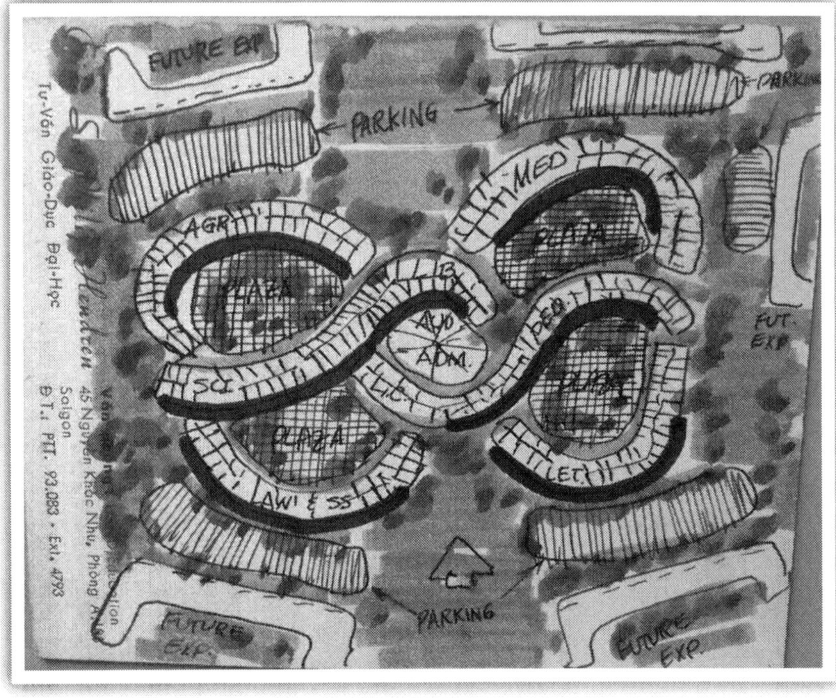
FUTURE EXP
PARKING
PARKING
MED
AGR
PLAZA
PLAZA
AUD
ADM.
SCI
L.C.
ED
PLAZA
PLAZA
LAW & SS
E.T.
FUT. EXP
PARKING
FUTURE EXP.
FUTURE EXP.

To deal with the issue of surviving in a war-torn environment, I suggested that we take a book from the British during the World War II blitz (and the Viet Cong) and build ventilated tunnels beneath and between the classrooms, laboratories, and housing.

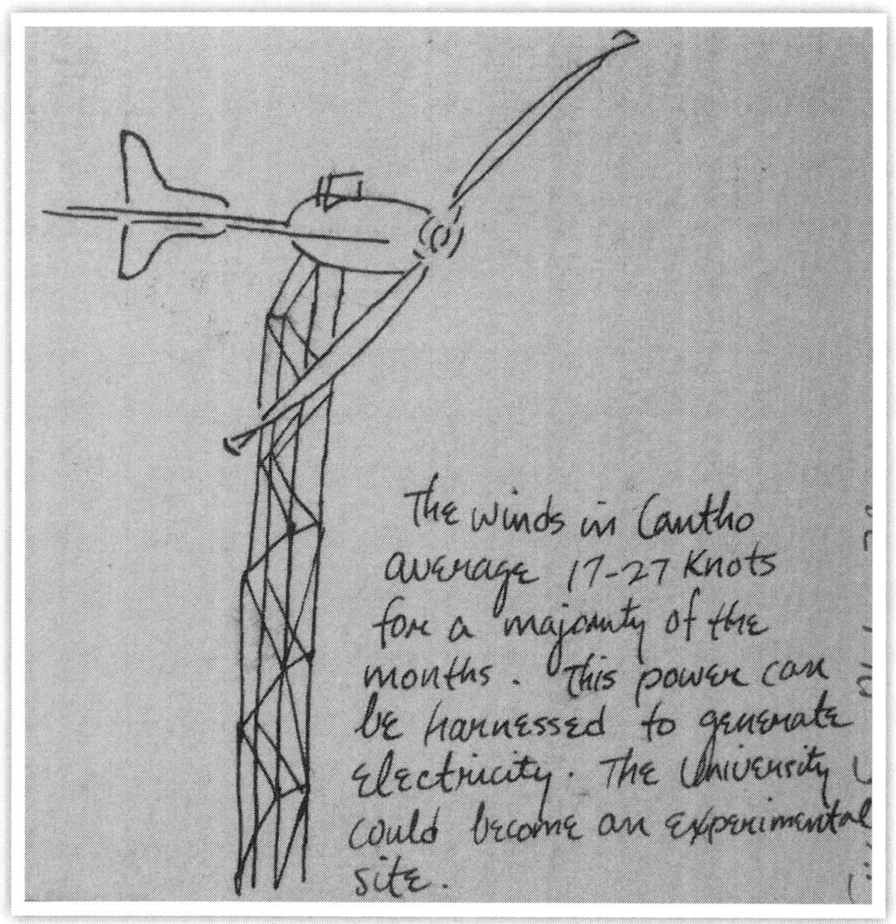

Wind and solar energy were emerging technologies that the university could explore and could help improve the economy of the community.

The following is from my diary:

"June 30, 1973: I am a naturalist by birth and believe much more can be achieved by 'planting' rather than 'planning.' Those who plan are nearly always disappointed, but those who plant are rewarded. The difference is one of attitude. 'Planting' implies allowing a natural process to take place while giving it direction and tending to its health. 'Planning,' on the other hand, means forcing an outcome conceived previously. It may seem outrageous to question the validity of 'planning,' i.e., it may seem like questioning the validity of thinking. Yet I am willing to take on the whole concept of planning on the simple grounds that 'it never works out that way anyway.' Let's assume that a worthy goal is the minimizing of frustrations in life…we would not only like to minimize them but would like to turn them into sources of pleasure. In 'planning,' an unforeseen event may be seen as troublesome or even disastrous. In 'planting,' it may be seen as just another challenge to be dealt with whatever is needed so the project can continue. So the idea is to plant (over-plant) without planning heavily on using the crops or allowing for many contingencies, any of which will be acceptable. If a flower comes up in the middle of your corn crop, treat it not like a weed."

I tried to say something like this to Rector Truong...that these sketches were just "seedlings." I told him his was the best opening address I had ever heard and that I felt it held important implications for the design of his new campus. He agreed, and we became great friends. He asked if I could help him with the design for a Japanese garden for his backyard.

We went to the Hue airport to catch a ride back to Saigon so I put lighter fluid in my Zippo and bought a pack of Winstons. Happily (or not), Air America put us on a C-47 paratroop carrier so I didn't have to worry about lighting the pilot's cigarette, but the thing was so shaky and rattled so much that I thought maybe they liked it that way so that the paratroopers would rather jump out than stay aboard.

THE SEARCHING

Setting: Mid-April 1975, River Oaks Farm, 2105 Scenic Drive, Austin, Texas (Unofficial Vietnamese Refugee Center)

River Oaks Farm studio & location of the unofficial Vietnamese refugee center.

Austin architect hates to watch S. Vietnam fall

By HOLLY HUDLOW
Staff Writer

Unlike many Americans, Austin architect Philip Hendren's tour to South Vietnam two years ago was a peaceful government mission.

In his year there, he made scores of South Vietnamese friends and grew to love the tropical countryside.

Now, through television and news reports, he is painfully watching the country crumble.

Hendren was one of the first architects involved in the United States' $3 billion reconstruction program in South Vietnam. He was hired by the U.S. Agency for

PHILIP HENDREN

The *Austin American-Statesman,* Sunday April 13, 1975:

It was mid-April 1975, and the news from Vietnam was bleak and getting worse. I was worried about the people still there who had been my friends and colleagues during the previous two years. I had written to several and offered assistance and whatever help I might be able to provide. The *Austin American-Statesman* published my picture with a group of orphans and an article entitled "Austin Architect Hates to See S. Vietnam Fall," which outlined my position on the state of the war.

I hoped that the stalemate would result in something like what happened in Korea. I thought we had left the ARVN (South Vietnamese army) powerfully equipped to defend themselves, and I believed my Vietnamese friends would somehow work themselves into positions of leadership in an emerging democratic republic of South Vietnam. I had been back only a few months, and I had seen the vast acres of tanks, half-tracks, howitzers, jet aircraft, ammunition dumps, and what I thought was a well trained militia able to utilize all that equipment. Little did any of us know that within a few weeks, by April 25, the whole picture would collapse into a chaos of total defeat for all of the Americans still there and all the Vietnamese civilians who had been our friends and allies.

On April 22 I received the following letter from my friend Vo Bach Phuong. She was not a bar girl or lover but a young music student I had been trying to help get a piano scholarship to come to the United States:

April 19, 1975

Dear Philip,

Thank you so much for your kind letter. I was very delighted to hear from you and I am very touched by your kindness.

Saigon is really getting worse. My family is still safe but we are all very nervous and worried. Everybody is most certain that Saigon will fall one day and we hope that day will be still far so that we can have enough time to leave the country. No one wants to live with the communists. But the serious problem is that our government forbids anybody to go abroad, except those who are married to foreigners. Still, people try to get out of Vietnam by many different ways such as buying or renting a boat, stealing an air plane, buying a passport or an exit visa for several millions piasters..., but most of them failed to escape and were arrested by the police and were put in jail. The only official way to get out is to sign a marriage contract. Many travel agencies combined with many american and french bachelors make a lot of money by signing marriage contracts with rich girls. I can get out by that way but I have to pay in advance 3,000,000 $VN and the great risk for everybody is to loose money and to get false papers and be put in jail.

I very appreciate your kindness to want to help me but I am afraid it will be hard for you. If you want to help me, you'll have to come to Saigon and sign a marriage contract with me, and I'll sign a promise to you that I'll sign a divorce contract right after we get out of

VN a any time you want. You don't have to pay anything for me. If you think you could do it, I'll be very happy and moved. I think it will be the greatest help in my life. But if you couldn't do it, I'll understand and I'll never be angry with you, however, I always appreciate your kindness to have remembered me and to have thought of helping me.

I have some american friends here, but I was so shy before that I never dared ask them for helping me. But when the situation seemed to be serious, I dared ask them and I was too late, they have promised to help other girls.

Anyway, if you receive this please write to me immediately. I'll be very impatient.

We have thought of a very small chance to be evacuated with the americans when such a situation arises because my sister and my brother in law Phiet know a lot of americans in Saigon, and they might help us. However, this is very uncertain, because all the americans might receive some day the order to leave, and they might be evacuated quietly at night like in Cambodia without letting anybody know. All the americans in Saigon are ready to leave at any time. They have all packed and sent everything home. American schools and university and others were closed. Most of the americans have left and are still leaving every day. That makes us so scared.

I'm waiting impatiently for your letter!

I hope to see you again very soon.

Very sincerely yours,

PHUONG

Who could say no to this? I immediately began preparations to go. Before leaving Saigon, I had been told that Pan Am was offering round-trip fares for half price; if you purchased them for cash you could travel from pretty much anywhere to anywhere at a huge savings. So I had purchased an open-date round-trip Austin to Auckland ticket with the hope of getting to see the myriad exotic sights of New Zealand within a year or two.

I called Washington to get the help of Ambassador T. C. Clark for a visa but was told that no visas were being issued to Vietnam for anyone. So I decided to hell with a visa and grabbed my ticket, passport, and USAID credentials and booked a one-way flight on Pan Am for Saigon leaving Sunday, April 25. The best connection required a four-hour layover in Los Angeles.

Somehow, Holly Hudlow of the *Statesman* found out about my plans and called to see if there was any possibility of an interview. I said there really wasn't, so she said, "How about just five or ten minutes on the phone and we'll air it on KLBJ?" After it aired that afternoon, my phone started ringing nonstop. I got Jerri McClarran to help answer the phone—she had become my friend and invaluable assistant with all the refugees that had been arriving that week to collect supplies that were pouring in from hundreds of generous Austin citizens.

Most of the calls were from GIs—veterans stationed at Bergstrom AFB who were worried about friends or relatives and wanted me to get messages to them. Before I left we had a list of over 250 names to look for and an equal number of names and addresses of potential sponsors for the refugees. Jerri agreed to stay at ROF (River Oaks Farm, my studio and home) and manage the chaos and be in daily phone contact—and take care of Dudley, my wonderful sheepdog-terrier. When I left, the courtyard at ROF was piled with mattresses, bedding, TV sets, clothes, boxes of dishes, and canned food, and the phone that would not shut up. (I should note that not all the calls were supportive or from generous donors or soldiers seeking lost lovers—some of them came from prejudiced bigots who would say something like, "You the one tryin' to bring them slant-eyed chinks to Texas?" or "You better not be helpin' them baby killers and their whores!") It was an emotional time, and I knew I was in the middle of a potentially disastrous entanglement. My guiding principle was the old Texas Ranger quote, "Do the right thing and suffer the consequences." I hugged Jerri and Dudley and took off for LA.

Polly Platt was a good friend because I had been a technical consultant on a movie she was making in Houston while I was teaching at Rice University. (She was well known for the movie *The Last Picture Show.*) It was called *The Thief Who Came to Dinner* with Ryan O'Neal and Jacqueline Bisset. Polly was the production designer and Bud Yorkin was the director, and they had needed someone to design a set involving lasers and gunpowder to simulate a thief burning his way into a glass case to steal the jewels. It was a minor part, but I loved the challenge. Polly and I struck up a close friendship. I was newly single and she had just divorced Peter Bogdanovich and had custody of their two gorgeous daughters who were about three and five. I had leased a furnished three-bedroom house near Rice from a physics professor who was on sabbatical, so when the little girls, Toni and Sashi, and their nanny showed up in Houston, I invited them all to share my house. Polly loved it since it had a play-yard and my dog Homer (a Great Dane); it was much better than a hotel. It had been a wonderful two or three months for us all.

So when I got to LA, I called Polly and told her I had four hours. She said, "By all means, get on over here!" She had since married another movie director, but he was away doing something and Polly and the girls were really glad to see me.

(It had been three years.) I filled Polly in on what was happening, and she said, "Oh my, what a story. I want to help, wish I could come with you. Please stay in touch. I'll do anything I can!." That was great encouragement to hear as I was on my own about to go somewhere "off-limits" again and into who knew what kind of hornet's nest.

Polly is a critical part of the story because I found out later that after I left she called Grace David in Houston (who had introduced us in the first place) and talked to Diane, Grace's daughter, who was also a great friend but didn't know what an adventure I had gotten into. Then Diane called my number in Austin and talked to Jerri, who filled in the rest of the details and told Diane she would contact her with updates as things developed.

As my Pan Am flight from San Francisco to Saigon was taxiing on the tarmac for takeoff, the plane abruptly stopped and the pilot announced that the war had escalated again and the Ton San Ute AFB and airport were being bombed. This flight was redirected to Guam where most of the Vietnamese refugees were going. The pilot said, "If you don't want to go to Guam please exit to the buses." A few passengers got off, but most like me were headed to Saigon to help the refugees and so decided to go on to Guam. I felt like everybody on the plane had a common goal, but nobody had any idea of what to expect.

When I arrived, I took a taxi to the docks to witness the first wave of what was to be a flotilla of ships, barges, and freighters teeming with people who mostly had nothing but what little they could carry and had consumed virtually no food or water for days. The US Navy and Air Force personnel from Anderson AFB were working frantically to set up dockside latrines, dressing shelters, and showers for the disembarking hordes. I started photographing the scenes until I ran out of film.

The following is from my diary:

"Guam, May 9, 1975: The faces incredible, smiling mostly, woman, riding in wheel chair, children happy, helping, playing, grinning at a new world and to them a great adventure. Very few but some seemingly complete families. Last boat took five hours to unload, 9:00 p.m. to 2:00 a.m. and we stayed until the last person was off, looking for Asia Foundation staff and friends. I'd been up since 4:00 a.m. and was exhausted by 11:00 p.m.…I climbed on top of a huge cylindrical trash container for a place to sit and watch…fell asleep and nearly fell off… climbed down thinking it would be bad form to break an arm falling off a trash can."

The following is another entry from the same day:
"To docks to watch three ships unload refugees…most powerful experience. First ship directly from Saigon River…was fired upon killing and injuring several. Thousands aboard coming down ramp in continuous line of seeming infinite length, carrying everything imaginable…most pitiful small bundles or tin cans. One man had a two-foot-high statue of Virgin Mary, one bicycle 'kid must be a genius' he grinned happily and rode his bike around the asphalt dock area!"

I began to realize that any chance of finding Vo Bach Phuong or anyone else on my list was pretty slim. A marine guard was stationed at a card table at every gangplank and getting the refugees to sign in with their names and ID numbers on yellow legal tablets. These were then transported to Anderson AFB where the data was keypunched onto IBM cards and printed out on an IBM 1620 computer. I was told I had to go to Anderson to see the lists, so that was the next stop.

The guards at the gate looked at my USAID credentials and lists of Vietnamese names and escorted me to the office of the commanding officer, Colonel Leo D. O'Halloran Jr. He saw me almost immediately and said he would do everything he could to help. He asked an aide to bring in the computer lists they had accumulated so far. When I looked at them I realized that they were not in any order other than the approximate time of arrival of reach refugee. But the names had not been collected in a consistent order so to find one person—for example, Vo Bach Phuong—you would have to look through all the pages of names starting with *P*, then the ones with *B*, etc. It would take days or weeks, and there were lines of people waiting to look at the lists. I said to the colonel, "Sir, my specialty at Rice University is teaching computer graphics, and my training at MIT was on an IBM 1620 just like yours. I'm a pretty good FORTRAN programmer, and I think I can write some software that could greatly speed up the search. It could check for all six combinations of three-part names and point the inquirer to the right page in a matter of seconds." He looked at me and said, "Sir, you are a godsend," and he ordered his aide to escort me to the computer center. He also provided a car and driver for the duration of my stay to take me to the tent cities to look for the people on my lists.

That week the US Navy and Air Force on Guam did everything possible, including the use of all typhoon emergency rations, to help feed, clothe, and cater to the needs of the thousands of refugees! They were totally heroic. I for one will never forget and never again be cynical about the capabilities of the US military when a humanitarian need arises!

When I got back to the hotel for dinner, there was a message to please call Diane David (at the time Diane owned and ran the David Art Gallery, probably the best in Houston). When I finally got through she said, "Polly had called and said you needed help. What the hell are you up to now?" When I described the situation she said, "Well, we are coming to help you!" By "we" she meant Cruiser "Cru" Rowland (an artist friend), Dupee (another artist we knew, DuPuis Bateman), and Marilyn Lubetkin, who was her best friend at the time and owned Oshman's Sporting Goods chain. I flopped into bed thinking, "Oh my, no matter how out of control a situation may be, it can always get a little more out of control!"

But this was a case of any help is better than no help. And these left-wing artists and intellectuals who had sort of fallen through the cracks of the overrich of Houston's River Oaks society were on their way to the middle of what was possibly the most horrific human calamity on the planet!

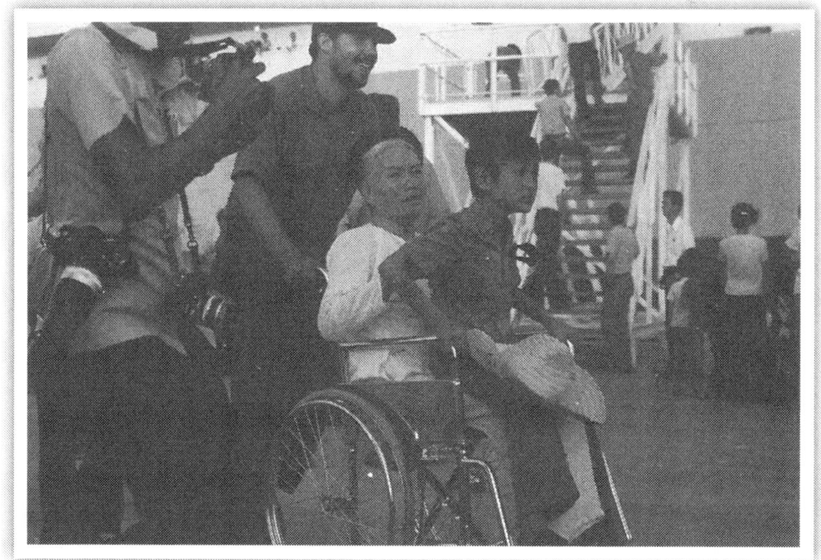

The following is from my diary:

"May 9, 1975: Guam declares general emergency, freeing up typhoon emergency provisions. To Red Cross to check lists, learn now people are being sent on to US without waiting for sponsors. Lists are incomplete…departure list inaccurate by 18,000! Actually it's incredible they are doing as well as they are. I traced Vo Bach Phuong to Orente Point, 'Tent City.' At Orente Point, have to get pass, drive up to top of Nimitz Hill for pass…no prob…Everyone cooperating, finally get to refugee station…40,000 in tent city, well named. A vast city of olive green dusty, smelly but could be much worse. Ran into Leroy Purifoy (ex-marine and friend of my brother, in Albuq.), who I had met before in Vietnam. He was one of the heroes during the April 25/26 evacuation days. LeRoy was looking for friends also and he said the best luck he'd had so far was to just walk up and down the tent city lanes and let yourself be seen.

Before I could get started a Vietnamese man from the Univ. of Hue recognized me…he said, "Rector Chau(my client for the design on the new campus at the University, Can Tho) was in Saigon April 29, I think he got out to Paris." I thanked him, left him my card, and promised him a sponsor. Then I found an Asia Foundation notice: "Contact Andrews, Hilton Hotel, Guam" [Andy Andrews, head of Asia Foundation, probably single most important American responsible for evacuation of friends and allies]. Drove to Hilton, unbelievable…looks like everyone on vacation [It is a favorite Japanese honeymoon hotel.]…Contrast shocking…the photos on same roll from refugee camp to luxury swimming pool at the Hilton!…should be interesting…stop judging…everyone has their own set of battles…most people really don't give a damn and that is their right…don't hate them, just look at what is. (San Miguel beer is excellent!) When I found the Andrews suite we compared notes. Andy and Eve (Andrews) seemed tireless and did find several friends and many acquaintances among the last refugees. They had had better luck finding people than I had but they needed more sponsors…I gave them my lists and we laid some plans for proceeding and staying in touch."

I went back to my hotel depressed, almost convinced that Phuong was no longer on Guam. I sent the following telegram:

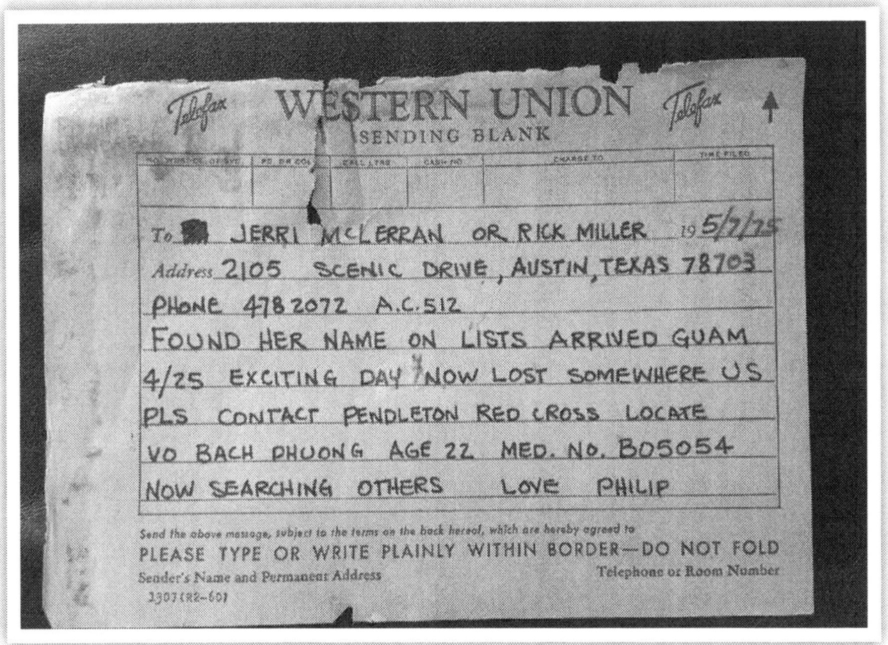
Telefax WESTERN UNION Telefax
SENDING BLANK

To JERRI McLERRAN OR RICK MILLER 19 5/7/75
Address 2105 SCENIC DRIVE, AUSTIN, TEXAS 78703
PHONE 478 2072 A.C. 512
FOUND HER NAME ON LISTS ARRIVED GUAM
4/25 EXCITING DAY NOW LOST SOMEWHERE US
PLS CONTACT PENDLETON RED CROSS LOCATE
VO BACH PHUONG AGE 22 MED. NO. B05054
NOW SEARCHING OTHERS LOVE PHILIP

Send the above message, subject to the terms on the back hereof, which are hereby agreed to
PLEASE TYPE OR WRITE PLAINLY WITHIN BORDER—DO NOT FOLD
Sender's Name and Permanent Address
Telephone or Room Number
1307(R2-60)

Photo of telegram with caption

The following is from my diary:
Guam, May 10, 1975: I was never so tired as when I finally returned to hotel to pick up car…to bed 2:00 a.m. with body, head, and soul aching. 4:00 a.m. phone rings, it's Cruiser Roland from Guam airport…A herd of Texas mavericks to the rescue!

Dear Philip —

The man at the desk said I could have a room (514) — Being a near relative of Greta Garbo I decided to take it — After all day with hundreds of people — I feel good with privacy — I know for a fact that you do too. We'll be back by 8:00 or so tonite So please don't go get a big Mac without us —

I hope I can still have Ritz + peanut butter privileges + we'll see you tonite —

Much love + XXXXX

D.

Early the next morning I found my driver and went to meet my friends at the airport. Marilyn had fallen sick and couldn't come but had made a substantial financial contribution to the effort. Diane, Dupee, and Cru hopped in the car and said, "Okay, what do we do first?" Diane gave me a peek into her purse with a wink and inside was a huge wad of hundreds, fifties, and twenties. It really cheered me up to see these three!

So I said, "Well, there are hundreds of kids in the tent cities with nothing to play with." So we went to every sporting goods store (only three) on Guam and bought volleyballs, nets, tennis balls, Frisbees, baseball gloves, bats, soap bubble kits—whatever anybody thought a kid would like. When the guys in the stores learned what we were doing, they gave us most of the stuff for half price and threw in a bunch of things they thought would help. Our only limit was how much the car would hold, so we had to go to the hotel, drop off bags, and make return trips. The rest of the day was spent delivering toys like midterm Santas.

The following is from my diary:

"Guam, May 12, 1975: Our driver said it was the best day of his service and that he thought there was nothing we could have done that would have been any more help with the morale in the tent cities! The next day we repeated the effort with transistor radios (all we could find on Guam), newspapers (the refugees had had no news for days), magazines, paperback books, art supplies, etc.

GUAM ELECTRONIC CENTER

P.O.BOX 2286, AGANA. GUAM 96910

TEL. 777-8830

No. 837-43 Date 5-12-1975

Name

Address

SOLD BY	CASH	C. O. D.	CHARGE	ON ACCT.	MDSE. RETD.	PAID OUT

QUAN.		DESCRIPTION	AMOUNT	
	1	TFM - 3750W	25	50
	2	Serial 225 235		
	3			
	4			

"May 12, 1975: Receipt for all the transistor radios in stock.

The system for people finding people was twofold…

"May 12, 1975: Found out the Chaus (Rector Chau, my friend and president of University of Can Tho) barely made it out of Saigon and now are in Paris. Remember story of his narrow escape from Da Nang on last barge from Hue. Rumors had it he disguised himself as a priest, wife Helun as nun, and children as orphans."

The system for people finding people was twofold: 1) put your name and the person you're seeking on a paper plate and pin the plate to a huge billboard set up for the purpose, and 2) stand on a raised platform at a PA system mike in the middle of a tent city and read names to the crowd.

I did both of these with limited success for the next two days while the Houston trio volunteered for the Red Cross and helped distribute medical supplies and pretty much whatever the Red Cross needed. They were just great, and I think to a person each felt it was the best thing they had ever done. Diane said it was even better than saving Pacifica radio (when a right-wing radical group in Houston had bombed the broadcasting tower of Pacifica radio because it was broadcasting antiwar news, she and a group of artists donated artwork and held a benefit auction, raising over $100,000 to get the tower rebuilt and Pacifica back on the air).

The following is from my diary:
"Guam, May 11, 1975, Mother's Day: Yesterday D., C., and D spent day at Anderson Red Cross serving food to outgoing refugees...' Dupee's Diner' beautiful day, all-time record beautiful sunset...as though God's reward for a day well spent...They/we must've opened a hundred thousand cans of C-ration, we heard it was the typhoon emergency food...the VN people coming through the food line: many children, few babies, or old people, no cripples or very few, all so gentle and always return a smile with a smile. Diane became 'medic' giving eye drops to kids with conjunctivitis. The paper plates were all converted into graphic art conveying messages of who is where or when or gone to Florida...all taped and stapled and made into a wonderful huge panel... it's much more attractive when mainly paper plates are the medium...it's like a design constraint within which there is great freedom."

It was in the tent cities where Diane's help was invaluable. She would not only read the names but also announce that anyone who had worked for USAID or who had worked for or attended the University of Hue or the University of Can Tho to gather at a table below the podium so we might find a connection to help them immigrate immediately into the United States. This led to connecting people to sponsors even though we didn't actually know them. We specifically asked if anyone knew of a pianist named Vo Bach Phuong or any member of her family. And we searched for anyone who might know Ye Thuong from Vung Tau or architect Ngo Viet Thu or any other architects and professors.

I was able to use my list of sponsors repeatedly in the different tent cities as I knew there was no way for the guards to cross-check, and anyway, they were as anxious to get the refugees out as were the refugees to get out. I was careful to notify everyone on my sponsor list of what I had done; I'd tell them that they might be receiving a call from a new Asian immigrant but there was no obligation, and if there was any problem at all to just send them to my unofficial refugee center in Austin. This never happened. I used all the names and addresses in my address book—many more than once—without permission to get as many people out of there as possible. Mostly they were people I had not actually known or seen but who looked okay to me and should be given a way out. One success story was a family that I sent to Albuquerque to my brother's address. The whole family worked in my brother's polystyrene factory for years, and they proved to be some of the best employees they ever had.

I had been told that if you were searching for friends you had known in Vietnam the best way was to just walk through tent cities and let yourself be seen. This turned out to be the best way for me, and I was able to find a few who recognized me. The best success I had in this was one afternoon when I had a sack full of transistor radios and magazines and was moving through offering them to each tent if they wanted them. A very pretty but disheveled lady who was my friend, Madame Le Van, was sitting on a bench. She looked at me and said, "I know you. You architect USAID, no?" I said yes and realized that she was the wife of the president of the University of Saigon and the personal assistant of Dr. Charles E. Rothwell, former president of Mills College and head of Ford Foundation project in Vietnam! She had been to dinner many times at the US Embassy and had been a great friend of Dr. Mary Neville (my boss) and was our connection to the school building programs in Bangkok. (See the story "Luck or Just Good Karma?") She was just a wonderful person, and I was shocked to see her in this camp, very lost with nothing but the clothes she was wearing!

I soon learned Madame Le Van's story. A few days before the fall of Saigon, Andy Andrews (head of Asia Foundation) was frantically working overtime to evacuate as many Vietnamese associates as possible because he knew their lives were in great jeopardy; in fact, anyone found to have been working with United States would be arrested and probably executed by the Viet Cong, and many were. Andy called Madame Le Van in her office and said, "I can get you on a flight to Singapore this afternoon, but you won't have time to go home and pack. I'll get word to your kids and husband and will get them to join you in Singapore as soon as possible." She agreed and left Saigon in great haste.

The next night alone in her hotel in Singapore she had serious misgivings about what she'd done and decided it was a mistake. She took the next available flight back to Saigon. She had no way of knowing her husband and children, Le Khiem (age thirteen) and Le An My (age fifteen), had left six hours earlier on a US evacuation flight. When she called for a ride from the airport and her servant answered, she knew immediately; she told me, "My bones froze on the inside." Miraculously, a soldier who had been one of her students at the university recognized her in the phone booth and said, "Madame Le Van, what are you doing here? It's very dangerous!" She explained and he said, "Don't worry. I can borrow a jeep and get you home." Traveling after the 8:00 p.m. curfew meant possibly being shot, so they drove on back roads with no lights and wore helmets and flak jackets. When they arrived at her house, the door was standing open and there was no electricity. The house had been ransacked and looted, all her clothes and many possessions were gone, and there was no sign of what had happened to her family. Imagine returning to your home to find your husband and children gone and not even any clothes to change into!

It was past curfew so her student/soldier/angel agreed to stay with her and help her find out what had happened. The next day was April 26 and the Viet Cong breeched the walls and set fire to the Embassy. The city was in chaos. Madame Le Van's last resort was a retired Australian general who had lived in Saigon since the days of the French. He was much admired for his military heroism and had friends in both camps. He said at his age he was staying put no matter who came out on top and that he could work with whatever developed. She knew he had been helping some of her friends escape, so they went to his house. He was shocked to see her but said he was helping a group of Catholic nuns that day to get on a barge bound for Thailand; maybe he could slip her in with them. They found her a nun's habit, and she got out that night under cover of darkness. To the day I found her in that tent city in Guam she had had no news of what might have happened to her family.

I said, "Don't worry. I'll get you out of here and we'll find them." I gave her a radio and the money in my pocket, and we went to the guard station to fill out the papers to get her on the next flight to the United States. Before I left I said, "Here's my diary. Write down your kids' names and ages and also your husband's info. I'll get back to the computer at Anderson and see what I can find." Before she left the next day I was able to tell her that her kids and husband were safe and probably at Camp Pendleton. She gave me a big hug and said, "Thank you, I never forget you."

The following is from my diary:
"May 15, 1975: Before I had left Austin I got a call from Prof. Alan Taniguchi (Dean of the School of Architecture at U.T. Austin) who offered all sorts of

encouragement. . .he had been an Asian refugee back in the forties when all the Japanese people living in the United States were imprisoned after Pearl Harbor. He said that if I happened to get near Manila would I please check out an international design competition for low-income housing in or near Manila Bay. So I booked a flight to Manila where there were also a lot of Vietnamese refugees and I thought I might get lucky. The Texas trio was having a blast and wanted to stay as long as they could on Guam so we parted, promising to stay in touch through Jerri in Austin.

"Manila was great but I only had one day so I got the data on the design competition and went by wildly colored taxi to see the site. I photographed it and thought this might be an opportunity to employ some of our design ideas from the two projects in Vietnam, the weather and materials being so similar. I picked up two registration forms and sent Alan a telegram that I thought we should do it. I hit the tent cities in Manila and Seoul, Korea, but mainly learned that the refugees were being processed quickly on to Camp Pendleton, California. I was exhausted and decided to go to Bangkok for some rest and check on my furniture project with Molinox.

"May 16, 1975: . . .flight arrived early morning so to the Oriental Hotel for breakfast and meet Phisit. Newspaper says US Air Force sank three Cambodian navy gunboats. . .Thai says seven. . .somebody tampering with the truth again! We went to John Fowler for the finest in fashion then ordered two pair custom bell-bottom levis. To meet Princess Chumphot who had graciously offered me 'Krishnavana House' on my previous visit. I stayed there but we had not actually met. She was an elegant woman in her midfifties, educated in Switzerland, caused the King to lose an eye in an auto crash racing to propose before her train was to carry her away. He lost. She was only seventeen at the time and unmoved by his efforts. He married another who cared for him in the hospital.

Anyway she eventually married and bore a daughter, Marsi. Now her husband is dead and daughter not close so she's devoted herself to her nephews...'Guy' and his brother who are both architects, educated in Brazil."

After the courtesies, she eyed me with a certain disdain and asked if I were an American. I grimaced and said, "The way things were, maybe it would be better if I were a Canadian." I asked if Phisit had explained my mission—no—so I briefly related what had developed in Austin and Guam. Her response was to suggest that I must be one of those American pacifists. I was noncommittal but supposed I was. She said, "My experience in World War II—the denounced pacifists were nothing but a lot of wasted effort—all came to nothing." I hedged on being a pacifist and resented being so generally categorized when the wars were so clearly incomparable. She obviously had a tape recording in her head on pacifism and was determined I should hear it. I listened. When she finished I asked, '"What is the alternative?" Without a pause to think oft an answer, she cried, "The alternative is to do what is right!" I replied, "Which is?" She said, "There is a right way to do things." Again I replied, "Which is?" She answered, "Well, the Americans, you Americans, always seem to have good intentions but then manage only to make a big mess." I had to agree but not until staunchly defending the reason we went to Vietnam in the beginning—my old JFK speech.

Then I discovered that the real reason for dislike of Americans had something to do with the general way Americans behaved in Thailand, with their air-conditioned cars and supercilious treatment of the people. It was the same way I felt in Saigon—the way we enslaved the people we were supposed to be helping defend their freedom. Importing American food and building American-style buildings that don't fit—and the PX! That maybe was the big key. Why did we need the PX? What a lot of trouble and corruption that one thing caused. She said, "That's true. Americans don't like living like Asians. They want to live like

Americans in Asia and have servants and wives and mistresses—that's true—it's the whole approach to helping that causes such resentment."

Then we shifted the conversation to the personal side. She seemed a little unnerved when I pointed out that I was up to no more than I would be if Thailand fell to the Communists and I came to help Phisit. In fact, we had set up an emergency plan just for such an event. I think she began to wonder who would come to her rescue if she were an evacuee or refugee. Then I told of the woman about her age in one of the Guam refugee camps who was sitting in the commander's office. She was crying and appeared to have been crying for some time. When I inquired I found she had been searching frantically for her husband's name on the huge daily computer listings of incoming refugees. This day she had found him, right age, right weight, right spelling, but when she telephoned the camp to which he was assigned, another man answered. From the conversation she knew this man had killed her husband and stolen his papers and money. It's the kind of despair that makes you realize that no one understands. The princess was visibly shaken and shuddered at the unexpected end to my story.

The refugee program in Vietnam had somehow caused a huge anti-American demonstration in Bangkok. I think because we, the United States, wanted Thailand to help us with the refugees, and the Viet Cong, the victors, wanted Thailand to help their cause.

The following is from my diary:
"Trouble in Bangkok, Saturday, May 17: Waited for Phisit but he got lost… will have to mail leather ball and clothes later. To American Travel across from US Embassy. Great timing! Must be 1,000 people shouting, loudspeakers, anti-American parade…really hostile. When I left cab two Thai security men

stopped their VW, got out and walked past me five paces...I'd put my Finland knife in my boot and as usual it got wedged against my skin...and I had to stop and fix it...it occurred to me if those guys saw that knife they might grab me... so I stood up and kept walking...limping. People glared at me like I was a criminal, a huge sign on the Embassy gate (closed and locked) said: "HOW MANY WARS DID YOU START TODAY?...under an effigy of Uncle Sam. Never felt such hostile vibes anywhere...can't believe this is the Bangkok I had known and loved! I limped into the American Travel Co., fixed my knife, and got my ticket...hoping it would take a long time so I didn't have to go back out there, or maybe the crowd would leave. Finally regained my courage with knife back in place and decided to be a photographer...I looked and dressed like one... so maybe...I took the case off the Nikon and went out deciding to click in the face of anyone who glared at me or molested me...it always works on prostitutes when they approach or try to stop you...and I wanted to get some shots of the Embassy Gate. My courage dissipated when I got back in the crowd and I thought, 'Jesus! Let's get out of here.' So I got in the first cab empty and said, 'Just go that way. I'll point.' He didn't understand but let me stay in the cab anyway and began driving. I made a note of his name. (Usually in Bangkok you tell the destination and arrive at a price before going.) This time it was any place, any price...just go! We managed to get circuitously to the Oriental Hotel and I gave Chiem 200 baht for saving my life. I still felt stared-at but recovered at the bar and decided to change my disguise from photographer to tourist. So I bought some bamboo geodesic domes that keep insects off food when you eat outdoors, and a flute for Philip and some beads for Philbert and Sandy and a hammock and carved wooden chimes. I decided the packages would make me look more like a tourist and less like the CIA...which worked...but then, where to?

"I've got too much to carry around all day so got a cab to hotel where luggage is in storage with bell captain. I'd already checked out and even though plane didn't leave until 7:00 a.m. Sunday. It's 5:00 p.m. Saturday and I have no hotel but I'd slept till noon and was determined to get away from Bangkok without another hotel bill. The massage parlors stay open till 3:00 a.m. And by then it'll be time to go to the airport. So I stored the packages with the bellman and went to look for some way to spend Saturday night in a hostile Bangkok...would've given $1,000 for a disguise that made me look like anything but an American. Ended up acting like an American by having a hamburger and going to two movies just to stay out of sight...*Harry and Tonto* in English with Thai and Chinese subtitles, and *Birds and Bees* in Thai with English subtitles. But fell asleep and missed most of last...had some great footage on animals making love with wonderful displays of affection and caressing. The big vicious looking male being teased and fondled by a really beautiful female. Then it's 11:30 so back to hotel and find Mr. Chiem Sooksri...a wonderful man... taxi no. 223....and made a deal...we'll put all my stuff in his car and go find a massage place...he'll wait for me and then drive to airport...all for 150 baht ($7.50)...a bargain because it usually costs $6.00 just for airport.

"Decide to quit worrying about money and pay the price for the best massage I could find...I was truly very lucky to be alive! Anyway, was saving hotel bill.

"May 19, Meet "Lek," Miss Vibool Fuded Foong, 134/4-6 Soi Nanatai, Sukhumvit, Bangkok Thailand., not only a beautiful girl but strong...if anything a bit too rough but first time for foot massage...two hours of finest recuperative therapy known and we become great friends and she wants to ride to the airport to see me off so I introduced her to my friend Mr. Chiem,...and the three of us set off. I'd asked him earlier if he had a girlfriend and he'd said, "No, too expensive; anyway I too fat, just taxi man"...but he looked okay to me and I thought maybe the two of them might be perfect for each other. She had a baby, American fathered, he had a job, so I told her what a good man he is, saved my life, kept my things safe in his car, loaned me 200 baht ($10.00) to help pay for massage...until I could cash a travelers check...and lived with and took care of his mother. Don't know if it worked, like to think so. She rubbed my leg all the way to the airport but of course had to ride back with him...Anyway it really felt like friends parting when I waved good-bye and I felt much better about Bangkok than I had twelve hours earlier.

"All that ended four hours before my Bangkok/Seoul, Honolulu/LA flight time so I slept three hours and started writing a letter to Phisit and damned near missed the plane...would have except they closed a section of the restaurant and kicked me out...I had to race and almost lost. On last leg met Stephanie Krebs...Social Anthropologist, filmmaker, Harvard/MIT 300 Highland Street, West Newton, MA 02165...PhD...Thesis on 'Nonverbal Communication in Thailand'...(I felt I'd just experienced a lot of that!)...and she speaks Thai and French.

"My experience: One of the greatest things to learn about the human race is that whenever you are on a mission to do something 'high-minded" or 'worthwhile' or 'truly idealistic' or 'heroic,' people seem to appear out of nowhere to help.

"Seems extraordinary to meet just at a time when I need just such a person to help with this Vietnamese resettlement program. We brainstormed from Honolulu to LA and she decided to get involved.

"May 20, Camp Pendleton: Tent city to Camp Pendleton with Stephanie who wanted to have a look at a refugee camp. Found Madame Le Van's three children and husband finally in Camp #5 after all-day hunt! Great to have Stephanie along as translator as many refugees speak fluent French but not much English. Le An My (age fifteen) was so glad to see someone who'd seen her mother that she was nearly in tears the whole time…all the kids are beautiful and we talked and laughed for an hour. I gave them books and newspapers (very precious in the camp) and a deck of Korean playing cards from Korean Airlines. Le Khiem (thirteen) recognized his mother's handwriting in my book and all of them got very excited as they recognized names of their friends on my list…even were able to tell me about some they knew had gotten out of Saigon. Le An My told Stephanie in French that a young mother had died in the camp from the cold… there were not enough clothes when they first arrived and everyone was very cold…but the 'Gendarme' (French for US officials) had said they did not die of cold…but they had nonetheless and the Vietnamese held a Catholic funeral for them right in the camp. I don't know where they were buried. A lot more refugees have died since this started than the press has reported.

"I was beginning to freeze myself and it started to rain and we were four miles from our car which the guards wouldn't let us drive in…we hitched a ride with an extraordinary character…age sixty, truck driver, twenty-five years married, divorced his American wife last year who he was very bitter against…she'd taken him for $350,000 and was a fat ugly bitch who in the first place hated people and ran off all his friends and customers…so he got so worked up talking about his ex-wife I thought he'd have a heart attack! Anyway he'd found a wonderful Vietnamese woman and four kids and he was marrying her…knew he wouldn't live forever but didn't want to live alone and anyway she'd get his social security and estate and he damn sure didn't want his ex-wife to have it and then he started in on her again…we really appreciated the ride.

"The searching was ending on a bittersweet note. We had not found Vo Bach Phuong, but we had managed to help a lot of people who really needed it and we had found Madame Le Van and helped get their family together. It seemed to make all our efforts worthwhile.

"Austin, May 21, 1975: An officer from the State Department called and said that they were sorry to be so late in responding to my pleas for assistance but that the staff had been really stretched and hoped things had worked out well for me. As I was giving him a quick report I figured out that this must be one of the two guys who had been tailing me since I left Guam. Possibly the link had come from the trio of Texas mavericks (who might have been guilty of an occasional toke of something illegal) because somehow the CIA suspected we had a drug-money angle working and they couldn't believe that we could throw that much money around helping penniless refugees for there not to be a for-profit illegal import scheme of some kind. There wasn't. The guy on the phone gave it away when I mentioned almost getting killed in Bangkok...He said, 'I know.' Guess he thought I'd feel better if I knew there was someone watching my back. I had sent the following telegram from the LA airport to Ambassador Clark:

"Dear T. C.,
Just couldn't wait any longer so have set off on my own to try to find as many of our friends as possible. Will greatly appreciate any help from your end. I have all those from my Vietnam journal plus 150 more friends and relatives of Austin citizens. Also have list of over 200 potential sponsors from Austin. Please cable any special requests or information %Hotel Continental, Guam."

Maybe that is who sent these two guys. I guess I'll never know, but instead of feeling grateful it just made me feel creepy. He then said I really should lay off this search because if she had gotten out of Saigon, she knew how to contact me. If she didn't and was still there and the North Vietnamese found out some American was looking for her, then that could be very harmful for her. I said, "Thanks, but I may have started an avalanche that I can't easily stop."

What I didn't say was that I was exhausted and broke. When my plane landed in Austin it was 9:00 p.m. and there was no money in my pocket for cab fare home. Happily my next door neighbor, Alan McCree, happened to be there picking up his daughter, so I thanked my rabbit's foot and hitched a ride. On the way we passed a huge concert going on at the UT campus auditorium. It was a Willie Nelson benefit for the Austin Symphony Orchestra! Where else but Austin?

I was really glad to see Jerri and Dudley. The trip had shaken my confidence but sharpened up my memory. The last thing I had jotted down was:

"Diary, May 21, 1975:

How many roads must a man walk down
Before you call him a man?
Yes, 'n' how many seas must a white dove sail
Before she sleeps in the sand
Yes, 'n' how many times must the cannon balls fly
Before they're forever banned?
The answer my friend is blowin' in the wind,
The answer is blowin' in the wind.

Yes, 'n' how many years can a mountain exist
Before it is washed to the sea?
Yes, 'n' how many years can some people exist
Before they're allowed to be free?
Yes, 'n' how many times can a man turn his head,
And pretend that he just doesn't see?

Yes, 'n' how many times must a man look up
Before he can see the sky?
Yes, 'n' how many ears must one man have
Before he can hear people cry?
Yes, 'n' how many deaths will it take till he knows
That too many people have died?
The answer my friend is blowin' in the wind,
The answer is blowin' in the wind."

Made in the USA
Charleston, SC
25 March 2014